FARM FORK FOOD

FARM FORK FOOD

A YEAR OF SPECTACULAR RECIPES INSPIRED BY BLACK CAT FARM

ERIC SKOKAN

PHOTOGRAPHY BY CON POULOS

KYLE BOOKS

Published in 2014 by Kyle Books
www.kylebooks.com
general.enquiries@kylebooks.com

Distributed by National Book Network
4501 Forbes Blvd., Suite 200
Lanham, MD 20706
Phone: (800) 462-6420
Fax: (800) 338-4550
customercare@nbnbooks.com

10 9 8 7 6 5 4 3 2 1

ISBN 978-1-909487-12-3

Text © 2014 by Eric Skokan
Photography © 2014 by Con Poulos
Book design © 2014 by Kyle Cathie Ltd

Project editor Anja Schmidt
Design Ketchup
Photographer Con Poulos
Food and prop styling Erica McNeish
Copyeditor Sarah Scheffel
Production Nic Jones, Gemma John
and Lisa Pinnell

Library of Congress Control No.
2014941852

Color reproduction by ALTA London
Printed and bound in China by C & C
Offset Printing Co., Ltd.

ACKNOWLEDGMENTS

Jill, thank you for chasing windmills
with me. Without your help and
understanding this book would
still be on our list of things to do.

Anja, thank you for your steady
hand and brilliant editing. I've
learned so much from you.

Con, Erica and Mark, I'm still
awestruck by working with you.
Thank you for your focus, comradery
and joy.

To Heraclio, Thomas, Jeff and
the rest of the kitchen crew, it is
an honor to work with you. Your
consistent pursuit of excellence
has made this book possible.

To Julia, Chip and Trisha, thank
you for being a part of the journey.
Your hundreds of contributions are
the jumps over the hurdles along
our way.

CONTENTS

Imagine two bustling downtown restaurants, four kids, 130 acres of farmed land, 250 varieties of vegetables, 3,500 gallons of mixed lettuces, 10,000 pounds of beets, 120 hogs, 140 sheep, 80 laying hens, 1,200 broiler chickens, 20 turkeys, 16 geese, the new cattle, Turkish livestock guard dogs and a llama named Belle—all are a part of a typical year on our farm/restaurant operation at the base of the Rocky Mountains. My wife Jill and I, along with our hardy, experienced farm staff, work year-round to keep it all going. It's a big operation with lots of moving parts. Somehow, whether it's a 500-year flood, devastating swarms of grasshoppers, or -14°F below-freezing temperatures, we've figured out how to grow spectacular food for our cherished guests in our restaurants. And we love it.

THE BIRTH OF THE FARM

Like all great journeys, this one began with a small step. Literally one step out the kitchen door, I planted a garden where I could grow all of the herbs and leaves that transform the dishes in our fine dining restaurant, Black Cat Bistro. It was a big undertaking, but the benefits showed almost immediately. The continual harvests of delicate, edible flowers, leaves and herbs were an inspiration and a source of pride. Immediately I saw a new vigor to my cooking—the food was easily better than anything I'd created in the last two decades as a chef. It was a new awakening.

Some paths do not become apparent until you are a ways down them. That was the case for our farm. The first year my kitchen garden was so successful that I dreamed and planned all winter long about what I would do the next spring. I put garden beds in every conceivable place surrounding our house and ended the next season with a third of an acre planted. It was an endeavor, but the yield was spectacular! During the peak of the harvest almost every vegetable on the restaurant's plates came from our own garden.

Gardening is hard work. I enjoy it and the quiet that comes with it. More than anything, though, gardening gives me an outlet to think differently about food. Its cultural importance and its sourcing (or the folly and hubris we make of it) hold greater weight when you are in between the rows in the garden. Farming taught me to love and value food all over again.

THE LIFE OF A VEGETABLE

From a chef's perspective, the life of a vegetable begins once the box is opened and ends with the finished meal. Cases of vegetables arrive on the morning delivery and get packed into refrigerators. Lettuce arrives in 6-pound cases, carrots in 25-pound bags, apples in 40-pound bushels. Cooks arrive for their shifts and begin to work on the prep list written by the chef the night before: cutting, chopping, slicing or julienning. The goal is always the same: be ready for dinner service on time. There is never time to consider the essence of the carrots—they need to be peeled and trimmed, not contemplated. For my first 15 years of cooking, such was the role of vegetables.

Then I took a job leading the kitchen in a historic 300-room hotel. On any given weekend during the season we would execute six 100-person weddings, plus another for 300. At the same time, the main dining room would do 200 covers. From the outside, one might reasonably assume that a big hotel operation would be overwhelming. That's not the case. Our industrial food system is geared toward making operations like this run like a top. Pre-peeled carrots ready to go for pre-made veggie dip, pre-cut cheese cubes for the cheese platters made a day ahead, pre-made salsas and dressings waiting in the wings, pre-portioned steaks lined up for a moment on the grill to be followed by a packaged sauce and pre-cut broccoli. In a big kitchen operation the cooks

need more pairs of scissors for opening pre-cut food baggies than knives for cutting. On my first day, there were 23 cooks, 6 knives and 43 pairs of scissors.

In my many years in the kitchen I had been surrounded by food and yet insulated from it. There, on the hotel's loading dock surrounded by pallets of food, I couldn't find anything that looked, smelled or tasted like food. Something inside me snapped.

If the chef only sees the vegetables from box to plate and the farmer only from seed to shipment, who has a better perspective? Neither. Gaining a depth of vision for food was the most profound change that my gardening time brought about. Pulling carrots, a few per week to check their growth, provides the opportunity to think about their whole life. Tiny and precious carrots become sturdy and rock hard at the end of a long season in the sun and it's a long, delicious life in between.

ingredients for my restaurant, freedom from a food system based on scissors, time to think about the vegetables away from the tyranny of the approaching dinner service and a bounty of new things to learn. Gardening and cooking were compelling me to wander down a different path.

MAKING IT THROUGH THE WINTER

Buoyant over the success of the garden and my growth as a chef, I was deflated by a question posed tableside in late summer: "What are you going to do this winter?" To be sure, I would be sad to not spend my mornings in the garden, tending the plants and dreaming up new dishes. The existential farm-to-table question ran through my head: what good is it for a restaurant to grow produce if it only shows up for a fleeting moment in the summer? Obviously, stating that "everything on the menu" comes from the farm is not possible. (So long coffee. So long lemons.) Over time the idea that "if it is possible to grow it for the restaurant, then we should" began to take hold. That was about 80% of what the diners saw on their plates. That meant the farm's size had to grow.

The jump from one third of an acre to three crossed many lines, the most obvious being the need for a tractor. Digging garden beds and planting by hand is simply not possible at this scale. Yet I had never driven a tractor. I had only hazy childhood memories of riding on my grandfather's lap on his tractor at the old family farm. It was hard to start and the source of countless explicatives from my grandfather. I was warned many times to stay well clear of the moving parts of this dangerous tractor. That, plus its loud, jolting movement was enough to cement a deep respect, bordering on outright fear, of tractors in general. And here I was contemplating a long partnership with one.

"B" IS FOR BUTTERCUP

Fate played its hand a few weeks later. On a Saturday morning, I read an online posting offering an International Harvester Farmall B tractor for sale. It was the same model as my grandfather's.

I am a firm believer that both inanimate and animated things need names. My old pick-up truck

TINKER, BUILD AND LEARN

At heart, both farming and cooking are similar in that they are thick with opportunities to learn. After 20 years of cooking, though, I had to search for new things to learn. Then, along came farming.

As it turns out, both my father and grandfather farmed, though neither were experts. They were engineers who loved to tinker, build and learn and those were traits they passed along to me. Here is a non-inclusive list of things I had to learn the first winter before I could start farming: how do all of the vegetables grow, what are the seed spacings and depths, how often to water, how often to thin the plants, how to design and build an irrigation system, how to install a 5-horsepower electric water pump, how long from plant to harvest for each type of vegetable, how to take and read a soil test and then amend the soil, and what about the earthworms? I jumped at the chance to learn new things.

The gardening years brought together all of the pieces: a love of food, a personal quiet, amazing is named Bessie, for example. It has suited her well when she's worked hard for me and surprisingly well when she's needed some convincing to keep going. (I find it much more dignified to have long, meaningful conversations with recalcitrant machinery when you can address them by name.) I contacted a group of name-creation experts—that is, my four children—and told them we needed a name for the new member of our family parked in the driveway. We tossed about names associated with the vernacular of faming. After Mavis and Hilda, it was decided that the tractor liked Buttercup best. My five-year-old said definitively, "B is for Buttercup."

"Undulating" is the charitable word to describe the look of the rows that first season. Driving a tractor is not easy and reining in Buttercup's wanderlust proved a herculean feat. Bumping along the rows, cursing the wobbly steering and the undersized front wheel that seemed to leap left or right around the smallest clumps of dirt, I was thankful for the deafening roar of the motor, which kept my wife and children unaware of my lapses in manners. At the edge of the field, they cheered as Buttercup and I completed each pass.

KID IN A CANDY STORE

Yet when it came to selecting varieties to grow, "kid in a candy store" is how I would describe my method. Surrounded by piles of seed catalogs with their stunning photography and mouth-watering descriptions, I wanted to grow everything. Each variety would be perfect for this, that dish, or another. Onto the seed list it would go. Meticulously building the first year's planting guide on a spreadsheet, I was stunned to see the final tally of 250 different varieties.

Interestingly, the farm's current total number of varieties still hovers around 250, but the criteria for choosing them is somewhat more refined these days. With a bit of experience, I've developed an eye for what will be great on my farm, and ultimately on the plate in our dining room. For example, my favorite tomato growing up was the storied red Brandywine, large and packed with flavor. My grandfather grew them and so did my father. I grew them the first three summers on the farm. Out of the hundreds of Brandywines I planted, I counted at best only a gallon of usable

fruits. Brandywines like warm days followed by warm nights that one sees on the coasts. Our farm, located at the base of the mountains, catches a flood of cool mountain air after dark, which refreshes our tender lettuces (making them sought after at the farmer's market). But it stops the tomatoes from ripening, especially the Brandywines. Small to medium tomato varieties work better on our farm, so I focus on those.

A SPECTACULAR BITE

I learned a lesson the first year in the garden: Time is one of the most important elements in creating delicious ingredients for the restaurant. Tasting the first ripe peas off of a vine one morning, I had goose bumps—they exploded with flavor! I harvested a few handfuls and hurried to the restaurant to start cooking. Along the way, I forgot to use the peas that night. Interestingly, the following day they tasted only okay, like standard supermarket peas. Their magic was gone. I formed another goal for the farm: only grow varieties that yield spectacular bites—and then get them into the restaurant quickly.

Much of the produce we see in supermarkets is grown to hold its shape during long transport and storage times, so "fresh" in the supermarket means at least two weeks old the day it is placed on shelves. "Spectacular bites" are lost in a very short period of time. Yet, that is where the magic is. Our farm fields are only a few miles from the kitchen's back door. Because of that I could choose varieties differently and have far better produce. Progress #9 peas, Shin Karuda carrots, Hailstone radishes, and Jericho lettuce are some that I think of as "lightning in a bottle" discoveries.

In addition to vegetables, we now raise Scottish Highland cattle, hundreds of heritage Tunis sheep, 1,200 free-range chickens and dozens of Red Bourbon turkeys. This menagerie came about because of a spectacular failure. During that first year growing vegetables, I did a really poor job of growing turnips. No amount of kitchen "creativity" could rescue them: no soup, soufflé, nor stuffing. Planted close enough together to look like turf when the turnips germinated, my experiment in growing at a larger scale yielded a mountainous pile of woody turnips fit for little other use than feeding pigs.

As the pigs were destined for the restaurant I had to choose the right breed. Foremost their meat had to be delicious. Next they had to suit our unique climate; the endless, strong sun coupled with extremes of heat and cold. I believe hogs should live in a natural environment, free to roam across wide pastures occupying their days rooting around for food. That meant a hardy, thrifty breed that could thrive when left to its own devices. Lastly, the hogs needed to be safe to work with. After hearing horror stories of farmers chased around by very angry and even hungrier hogs (and since I am not the most fleet of foot), a calm, gentle disposition was prominent on the list.

The American Livestock Breeds Conservancy conducted a blind taste test of both heritage and commercial hog breeds. The winner was the American Mulefoot hog. I looked a bit deeper into its traits. Long black hair and black skin meant it could handle sun, heat, snow and wind. Check. I learned from breeders of its gentle nature. Check. Some thought it was naturally immune to most hog diseases. Check.

We located stock a few hours away and nervously headed off with our trailer in tow. While I had cooked pieces of pork for decades I was unprepared to see the boar, Alex, the tusked woolly mammoth of a hog that would be the head honcho back at our farm. "Oh my god. What are we doing?" were my first words. "Is he safe?" I asked Ron and Lynn, who would become our mentors in farming far beyond just the pigs at hand. "Oh sure. Just don't feed him by hand," Ron said with a chuckle.

The restaurant has always set the direction for the farm. When looking toward an expansion of the animal operation, we started with a look at what we bought for the restaurant from other sources. Now, seven years later, most of our meats come from our farm.

EVER EVOLVING MENUS

Writing menus before I had a garden was an exhaustive process—piles of cookbooks, hours of research and test runs culminated in the unveiling of a new menu. Next step was creating production efficiencies and honing the dishes. Then, I could let the menu run its course for a couple of months until changes in the season dictated a new one. In a year, there might be four or five complete menu changes.

Once I started farming, something different happened. In the middle of a menu run, I'd pull something really exciting, like scarlett runner blossoms or green coriander berries from the garden, something too good to leave off the plate. I'd make an update to the menu and the impact was startling: The dishes changed from well composed to alive. Soon, changes were coming more frequently and I ran dishes for shorter and shorter periods of time. By the end of that year, creating menus had become dynamic and ever evolving. The dishes were better and I was happier.

I had built a level of trust in myself to create great dishes based on what was available from the rows, not on importing ingredients from far away. Prior to the farm, ingredients were like clay to a potter, things I molded into ideas. Some dishes might be an examination of an old classic preparation fallen into obscurity or perhaps a humorous notion like "Duck, Duck, Goose!" In modern kitchens, chefs follow a dogma of cuisine. Certain flavors always go together:

"peas and carrots," "tomato and basil," and "fennel and citrus." They are delicious. But, they are also a well-trodden path. Farming led me down a different one.

INSPIRING INGREDIENTS

It was a June morning when I noticed that the cilantro had begun to bolt. I had intended it for an Asian inspired pork salad that would certainly not happen if the cilantro was all stems and flowers. Nipping off a delicate white flower to taste, it exploded with the flavor of cilantro. Only it was better: a gorgeous, clean, vivid cilantro. Immediately the possibilities for using them ran through my head: a salsa, a little salad on grilled chicken. But more important was the next thought, "How can I put this on the plate as simply as possible?" It was clear that complicating the dish would lessen its impact. In fact, I realized I only needed to get out of this flower's way so I didn't screw it up!

In the end, ingredients that come right off the farm—whether it's mine or from a local farmer—are good enough to stand on their own. When you have inspiring ingredients to work with, truly stunning dishes don't require a chef—just someone in the kitchen who is willing to get out of their way.

Think of this cookbook as a guide for aspiring gardeners or to your local farmer's market. The recipes are meant to be flexible, to help guide the inspiring produce you find toward the table. Better yet, they are a vision of what is possible one step out the door into the kitchen garden.

TYPES OF SALT AND OIL

I use several types of salt. Sel gris (gray sea salt from France) for seasoning meats, fish and vegetables; kosher for baking beets and seasoning water; and finely milled sel gris for salads and leaves (as it does not have a grit, which can be confused with dirt in a salad). However, I've only listed sea salt in my recipes for simplicity. For the same reason, I list sunflower oil in my recipes, but grapeseed oil could also be used—both have high smoking points and don't lend a taste to the wonderful ingredients you are cooking.

OVEN TEMPERATURES

Given the right conditions, braising meat is a simple process of browning and then cooking the meat in a flavorful broth, which becomes the sauce for the dish. It is often a one-pot recipe that's far better than the effort it takes to make. Unlike cooking a steak, where the window of time for juicy perfection is rather narrow, braises are very forgiving with a broader window. A few common mistakes can yield tough results, however. The temperature of the cooking liquid is critical. If it's too low the braise will be tough or chewy, so simply give the braise a quick temperature boost at the end of cooking to push it into the window. More difficult to correct, however, is a braise that is too hot. While it shortens the total cooking time needed to make the meat tender, it also shuts the window of time where the braise is tender *and* juicy. Once the meat goes through that window, it will be dry. My life at the farm and restaurant has gotten in the way of a good braise too often to chance it any longer. So now I set the oven at a low temperature and give it plenty of time.

I have a few more bits of advice. First, I've learned that most meats braise best when their cooking liquid is held at 180 to 185°F. That's the temperature where collagen, the meat's connective tissue, melts to a juicy tenderness. As everyone's oven is different, you'll need to experiment to find the setting that yields the right braising temperature. I recommend taking the time one cold weekend day to tinker with your oven as follows: Bring an ovenproof pan of water to a boil on the stovetop, and then cover and transfer it to the oven preheated at 200°F. Check the water temperature after 30 minutes and adjust the oven to get the water temperature to hover between 180 and 185°F. That will be your oven's best braising temperature, regardless of what a recipe says. Other options are braising on the stovetop (if your burners can be lowered enough to hold the right temperature) or using a crockpot. Lastly, I recommend that you heat the braise on the stovetop just until it boils, then cover and transfer it to the preheated oven. A cold pot with cold meat and cold stock may take more than an hour to come up to temperature in the oven.

SOURCING FAT

Animal fat from duck and pork are an unwanted by-product of the butchery process. Yet it is indispensable in many recipes. I suggest asking your local butcher for some to experiment with; most will be happy to sell you something they normally throw out. Most fats can be used interchangeably, but each has subtle differences. Beef fat, or tallow, has a neutral flavor and a very firm texture whereas pork and duck fat are soft and silky. Lamb fat carries a subtle but noticeable aroma; it makes other foods taste like lamb. When making sausage, use only raw fat as rendered fat can leak out when exposed to the barest amount of heat.

Caul fat is a paper thin, lacey layer of fat surrounding the animal's stomach. Used as a wrapper or purse, it is thin enough to melt away during cooking while imparting a bit of juiciness. It is a special-order item from your butcher.

WASHING AND DRYING FRESH PRODUCE

This should be obvious, but wash all fresh fruit and vegetables thoroughly and pat dry. To wash fresh herbs or flowers, I recommend slushing them around in a sink filled with cool water.

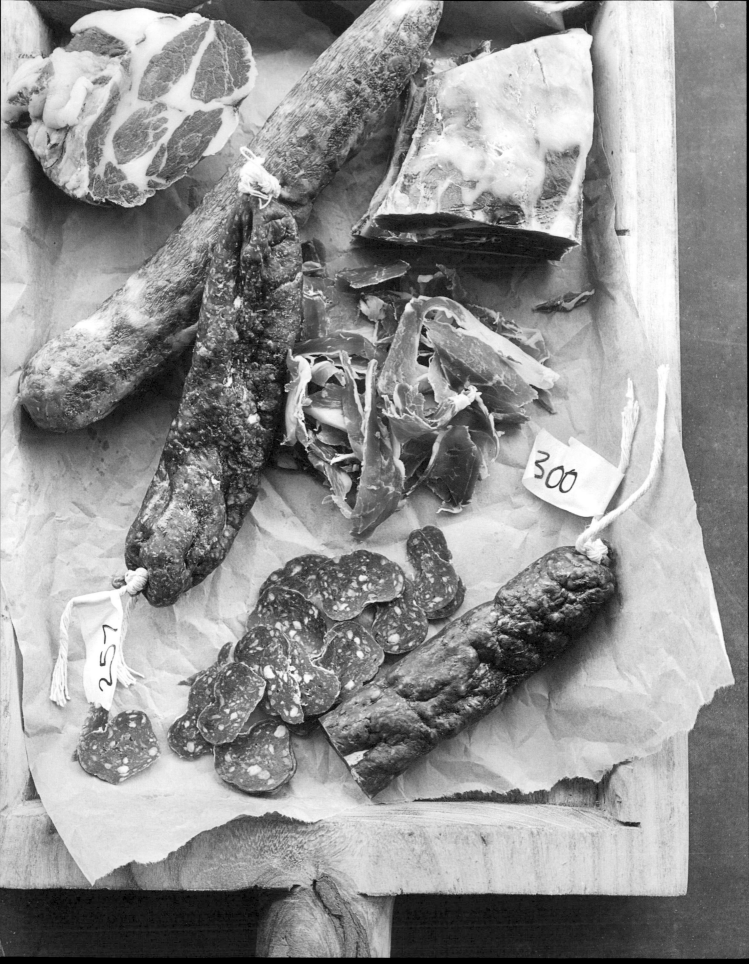

CHARCUTERIE

IN THE WORLD OF KITCHEN GADGETS, IT'S RARE TO NEED A MEAT GRINDER FOR ALMOST ANY RECIPE. IN THIS CHAPTER IT IS ESSENTIAL. FOR OCCASIONAL MEAT GRINDING AND SAUSAGE MAKING, I RECOMMEND A GRINDING ATTACHMENT FOR A STAND MIXER. FOR THOSE LIKE ME WHO LOVE MAKING SAUSAGES, I SUGGEST A STAND-ALONE UNIT. EITHER WAY, THE GRINDER EQUIPMENT SHOULD BE PLACED IN THE FREEZER THE NIGHT BEFORE FOR BEST RESULTS.

GOOSE LIVER PÂTÉ
WITH PICKLED CARROTS & MÂCHE

Silky smooth and rich, goose liver pâté is a pleasure and worth every bit of the extra effort in sourcing the livers. Here, I've paired it with tiny pickled carrots and mâche, one of the very first salad greens of the year at our farm.

SERVES 4

12 baby carrots, trimmed
sea salt
1 cup apple cider vinegar
1 tablespoon sugar
2 sprigs fresh tarragon
1 pound goose liver, soaked in
    water overnight, rinsed and
    patted dry
½ cup minced onion
1 tablespoon minced garlic
1 cup plus 1 tablespoon
    unsalted butter, softened
pinch of cayenne pepper
pinch of freshly grated nutmeg
freshly ground black pepper
3 tablespoons Calvados or
    other dry brandy
¼ cup heavy cream, warmed
2 tablespoons minced fresh
    chervil
1 cup mâche
2 teaspoons basic vinaigrette
    (see larder)

In a small bowl, combine the carrots with a liberal seasoning of salt and let stand for 20 minutes. Rinse the carrots well with cool water to remove the excess salt and place in a heatproof bowl.

Meanwhile, in a small saucepan over high heat, combine the vinegar, ¼ cup water, and sugar and bring to a boil, stirring until the sugar dissolves. Pour over the carrots and add the tarragon. Marinate for at least 1 hour.

In a large heavy-bottomed sauté pan over high heat, sauté the liver, onion and garlic in 1 tablespoon of the butter until the liver is pink in the middle, about 8 minutes. Transfer the liver to a platter. Return the sauté pan with the onion and garlic to the heat. Add the cayenne, nutmeg and a grind of black pepper and cook for 1 minute. Pour in the Calvados and deglaze the pan, about 3 minutes. Remove from the heat and add the remaining 1 cup butter, stirring until melted.

Place the liver and the onion mixture in a food processor and purée until very smooth, about 3 minutes. With the motor running, slowly add the warm cream and purée until smooth. Transfer the pâté to a mixing bowl and chill in the refrigerator for at least 1 hour.

Remove the pâté from the fridge and add the chervil. Season with salt and mix well.

In a small bowl, mix the mâche and vinaigrette. Season with salt and toss well.

Divide the pâté among four small plates. Garnish with the pickled carrot and dressed mâche. Serve immediately.

COUNTRY PÂTÉ WITH TURNIP MOSTARDA

Pork pâté is a mainstay at our casual farmhouse pub, Bramble and Hare. Served with crusty bread and our zesty turnip mostarda, it is perfect for starting off a meal. This pâté takes to most pickled vegetables, though, so let your imagination or the farmer's market guide your choice. Plan ahead: You'll need to soak the pork liver and freeze your grinder equipment overnight.

SERVES 12

½ pound pork liver, cubed

1 pound pork shoulder, cubed

1 pound pork belly, cubed

1 medium onion, minced plus
　¼ cup julienned onion

1 cup roasted garlic
　(see larder)

2 teaspoons freshly grated
　nutmeg

1 teaspoon ground cinnamon

2 teaspoon ground anise

sea salt

freshly ground black pepper

¼ cup heavy cream

1 large egg

½ cup shaved turnips

2 tablespoons shaved garlic

½ cup Champagne vinegar

1 tablespoon mustard seeds

2 teaspoons sugar

A day ahead, soak the pork liver in several changes of cold water in the refrigerator. Pre-chill the meat-grinder attachment, auger and cutting dies in the freezer overnight.

Preheat the oven to 300°F.

Rinse the liver and pat dry. Pass the liver, shoulder, belly, onion and roasted garlic through the grinder set with a medium cutting die. Change the die to the smallest one available, then pass the pork mixture through the grinder a second time. Transfer to a large bowl and add the spices, 1 teaspoon salt, a grind of pepper, the heavy cream and egg and mix well.

In a small sauté pan over medium heat, fully cook 1 teaspoon of the pork mixture to judge the seasoning. Taste and add more salt and spices if necessary.

Lightly oil the inside of a terrine or shallow baking dish. Fill the terrine with the pork mixture and smooth the top. Cover the terrine and bake in a water bath until the internal temperature reaches 155°F, as measured by a meat thermometer. Remove the terrine from the oven and let cool, then refrigerate until well chilled.

In a heatproof bowl, combine the shaved turnips, julienned onions and 1 tablespoon salt. Marinate the turnips until they begin to sweat, about 10 minutes. Rinse off the excess salt with cold water, dry the turnips and return to the bowl.

In a medium saucepan over high heat, combine the garlic, vinegar, mustard and sugar. When the mixture reaches a boil, pour it over the salted turnips and let marinate until cool. Store the turnips in an airtight container in the refrigerator.

Arrange the chilled terrine and turnip mostarda on a platter. Serve with crusty bread.

LAMB MERGUEZ WITH ALMOND TARATOR

The famous sausage of Morocco, merguez is my favorite of all sausages. Richly perfumed with spices, it adds an exotic touch. We use it as a stuffing for poultry, as a winning appetizer or served simply with a garlicky almond sauce in this dish.

SERVES 6

1 pound lamb shoulder
¼ pound lamb fat
½ cup minced onion
3 tablespoons minced garlic
2 tablespoons paprika
1 tablespoon ground cumin
1 tablespoon ground coriander
2 teaspoons fennel seed
1 teaspoon ground caraway
1 tablespoon minced
   lemon zest
2 tablespoons lemon juice
¼ cup chopped fresh cilantro
sea salt
¼ cup almond tarator
   (see larder)

Pre-chill the grinder attachment, auger and cutting dies in the freezer overnight.

Pass the shoulder, fat, onion and garlic through the grinder set with a medium cutting die. Change to a small die and pass the lamb mixture through the grinder a second time. Transfer the mixture to the bowl of a stand mixer fitted with a paddle attachment. Add the spices, lemon zest and juice and cilantro. Season with salt and beat on medium speed until tacky, about 3 minutes.

In a small sauté pan over high heat, fully cook 1 teaspoon of the lamb mixture to check for seasoning. Taste and adjust if necessary.

Form the merguez into 1-inch balls, or kofti. Cook in a large sauté pan over medium heat, 3 to 4 minutes per side.

Divide the merguez kofti among six small plates. Garnish each with the almond tarator and serve immediately.

PORK CHORIZO WITH AVOCADO & CILANTRO

Chorizo made from scratch is not only rewarding but substantially better than the store-bought version. Very versatile, it is used for everything in our kitchen. Here I've paired it with refreshing avocado and cilantro. Any leftovers are wonderful scrambled with eggs in the morning.

SERVES 4

1 pound pork shoulder, cubed

4 ounces fatback or pork belly, cubed

¼ cup diced onion

2 tablespoons minced garlic

2 tablespoons ground chiles de árbol

1 tablespoon ground black Oaxaca chiles

2 tablespoons ground coriander

1 tablespoon lemon juice

sea salt

1 cup fresh cilantro leaves

1 avocado, peeled, pitted and diced

2 tablespoons julienned red onion

juice of 1 lime

2 teaspoons sunflower oil

Pre-chill the grinder attachment, auger and cutting dies in the freezer overnight.

Pass the shoulder, fatback, onion and garlic through the grinder set with a medium cutting die. Change to a small die and pass the pork mixture through a second time. Transfer to the bowl of a stand mixer fitted with a paddle attachment. Add the spices and lemon juice and season with salt. Beat on low speed until tacky, about 3 minutes.

In a small sauté pan over high heat, cook 1 teaspoon of the pork mixture to check for seasoning. Taste and adjust if necessary.

Form the chorizo into 2-inch diameter patties. In a large sauté pan over medium-high heat, cook until lightly browned, 2 to 3 minutes. Turn the patties over and cook for about 2 minutes more. Transfer to a platter to rest.

In a small bowl, combine the cilantro, avocado, red onion, lime juice and oil. Season with salt and toss lightly.

Divide the avocado salad among four small plates. Top with the chorizo patties and serve immediately.

CHILES

Of the hundreds of types of chiles and chile powders I prefer the ones that are light on heat but long on flavor. Tops in my book is the black chile of Oaxaca and the tobacco-scented Ancho chile. A trip to the local Latino market is the trick for sourcing the best dried chiles. Sometimes you'll find tortillas still warm off the tortilla press there, too! Substituting regular chile powder is a possibility, just insist that it is very fresh and fragrant.

PORK HEAD CHEESE TERRINE
WITH OUR CORNICHONS

For the adventuresome cook, this is a delight. Despite the odd name, this traditional terrine is simply made from the rich meat of the pig's head, set with a stock and flavored with herbs. Ask your butcher or a local farm for a pork head, which needs to marinate overnight. We grow tiny de Bourbonne cucumbers, the variety traditionally used for producing cornichon pickles.

SERVES 4

1 pork head
1½ cups salt, plus more
   for seasoning
¼ cup sugar
6 fresh bay leaves
20 black peppercorns
4 cups ice
2 cups white wine
¼ cup fresh thyme leaves
1 cup minced fresh parsley
¼ cup roasted garlic
   (see larder)
¼ cup sherry vinegar,
   or to taste
freshly ground black pepper

FOR THE PICKLES

2 cups cornichon-style
   cucumbers
2 tablespoons sea salt
1½ cups champagne vinegar
1 tablespoon sugar
4 bay leaves
1 tablespoon juniper berries
1 tablespoon mustard seeds
1 tablespoon coriander seeds
1 tablespoon crushed red
   pepper flakes

One day ahead, soak the pork head in several changes of cold water, until the soaking water is clear. In a medium pot, combine 2 quarts water, the salt, sugar, bay leaves and peppercorns. Heat the water over medium, just until the salt fully dissolves. Add the ice and stir until it melts and the brine is cold. Place the pork head and brine in a large plastic bag. Expel any air to insure that the head is fully submerged in the brine; seal and place in the refrigerator to marinate overnight.

The next day, remove the head from the brine and discard the brine. In a pot just large enough to accommodate the head, combine it with the wine and enough water to cover. Season lightly with salt and bring to a boil over medium heat. Reduce the heat to a bare simmer and cook until the meat falls easily from the bones, at least 6 hours.

Remove from the heat and let cool. Strain the head through a colander, reserving the broth. When the meat is just cool enough to handle, remove the bones. Chop any large pieces of meat or tissue and transfer to a medium bowl. Add the herbs, roasted garlic and vinegar, season with salt and pepper and mix.

Line a terrine with plastic wrap. Fill with the pork mixture and tap the mold firmly on the counter to settle the pork and remove any air pockets. Slowly pour the reserved broth over the pork to fill in any remaining gaps. Chill the terrine in the refrigerator until fully set, about 2 hours.

Meanwhile, make the pickles: In a heatproof bowl, toss the cucumbers with the salt and let stand for 20 minutes. Rinse well with cool water to remove the excess salt. Return to the bowl.

In a small saucepan over high heat, combine the vinegar with ½ cup water, the sugar and spices. Bring to a boil, then pour over the cucumbers and let marinate for at least 1 hour.

Remove the terrine from the mold and unwrap and discard the plastic. Cut into ¾-inch-thick slices. Divide among four small plates and garnish with the cornichons.

RENDERED LARD
Rendered lard is made by slowly cooking finely chopped pork fatback in a pot with equal parts water over low heat. Cook gently until the water evaporates, roughly 1 hour per pound of fatback. The water prevents the fatback from coloring, resulting in a pearly white lard with no porky flavor. It is also available already rendered from your butcher.

PORK RILLETTES WITH HORSERADISH

For those interested in learning to make charcuterie, pork rillettes is a great place to start. Because the first part of the process yields confit pork shoulder, I suggest doubling the recipe and making the rillettes with half. The extra is perfect for making pork confit with ginger gastrique, page 108.

SERVES 12

2 pounds pork shoulder, cubed
sea salt
1 quart rendered lard
    (see note, above)
1 orange, halved
2 bay leaves
2 cinnamon sticks
1 teaspoon freshly grated
    nutmeg
1 teaspoon ground allspice
freshly ground black pepper
¼ cup sherry vinegar
freshly grated horseradish

Preheat the oven to 180°F. Season the pork liberally with salt.

In a heavy-bottomed braising pan over low heat, combine the pork, lard, orange, bay leaves and cinnamon. Cook until the lard melts and begins to boil, about 15 minutes. Cover the pan with a tight-fitting lid and transfer to the oven. Cook until the pork is very tender, about 5 hours.

While still hot, remove the pork from the fat and coarsely chop. Reserve the melted fat. Transfer the chopped pork to a stand mixer fitted with a paddle attachment. Add the remaining spices and vinegar and mix on low speed to break up the pork. Add ¼ cup of the reserved fat, increase the speed to medium and mix for 1 minute. Taste the pork for salt and adjust if necessary.

Transfer the pork rillettes to clean glass jars. Top each jar with melted pork fat to protect the surface of the meat. Chill in the refrigerator overnight or up to several weeks.

To serve, spread the rillettes onto crusty bread or toast. Top with the fresh horseradish to taste.

SOUPS

MAKING THE PERFECT SOUP BALANCES TWO COMPETING GOALS: CREATING FLAVORS THAT COMFORT AND CREATING FLAVORS THAT EXPLODE. I LOOK FOR INGREDIENTS THAT RESONATE WITH DEEP FLAVOR FOR THE STARTING POINT OF ANY SOUP. THEN I ASK, "HOW DO I MAKE THIS SOUP JUMP?" THAT'S THE ROLE OF THE FUN GARNISHES ADDED AT THE END. THIS COMBINATION OF GOALS YIELDS SOUPS THAT ARE AT ONCE HOMESPUN AND ELEGANT.

SPRING PEA SOUP
WITH MINT, LEMON & CRÈME FRAÎCHE

When our farm's peas arrive in sufficient numbers to make the first bowls of this soup, I know farming season has arrived in all of its glory. I prefer shell peas for this soup, as they have enough body to yield a creamier texture. Better yet are petit pois—spring peas harvested very young and tender. All parts of the plant find a use: blanched peas add body and a fresh "pop," shells are juiced to deliver flavor and depth, and flowers and tendrils yield a spectacular garnish. I serve this hot or chilled to suit the weather outside.

SERVES 4

1½ pounds shell peas, shucked
reserved pea shells
1 medium onion, diced
3 cloves garlic, chopped
1 medium potato, peeled
   and diced
1 quart vegetable stock
   (see larder)
8 ice cubes
¼ cup crème fraîche
sea salt
lemon juice to taste
¼ cup mint leaves, julienned
12 pea flowers
6 pea tendrils
1 tablespoon lemon zest,
   finely julienned

In a medium saucepan over high heat, blanch the shucked peas in boiling salted water until their color brightens, 20 to 30 seconds. Strain the peas and immediately plunge them into a bowl of ice water. After the peas have chilled, strain and set aside.

In a medium saucepan over medium-high heat, combine the reserved pea shells, onion, garlic, potato and stock. Boil until the stock is reduced to three-quarters of its original volume and the potato is very tender, about 40 minutes.

Transfer to a blender or food processor. Add half of the reserved peas. Blend until velvety smooth, adding water if the soup is too thick to easily purée. Strain through a fine strainer. Add the ice cubes and crème fraîche and stir until the ice cubes have melted. Season with salt and lemon juice and place in the refrigerator to fully chill, about 1 hour. To serve the soup warm, return it to the saucepan and warm fully over low heat, 10 to 15 minutes.

Divide the soup into four soup bowls. Top each with the mint leaves, pea flowers and tendrils, and lemon zest. Serve immediately.

COOKING TIP

When making a chilled soup, I always add ice cubes at the end of the cooking process. The ice both cools the soup quickly and thins it out. It's also a great trick when making green vegetable soups like peas and asparagus as it helps keep their color brighter.

HEIRLOOM CARROT SOUP WITH COCONUT MOUSSE

This simple soup combines only three elements: carrots of rich flavor, velvety coconut milk mousse and the perfumed crunch of candied lime zest. For an easier but equally delicious soup, substitute a healthy squirt of fresh lime juice for the zest.

SERVES 4

2 medium onions, julienned
1 tablespoon sunflower oil
6 cloves garlic, sliced
1 pound carrots, peeled and chopped (see note, page 145)
4 cups coconut milk
sea salt

4 fresh lime leaves
2 tablespoons lime juice
1 tablespoon sliced fresh ginger
1 teaspoon ground dried shrimp
2 tablespoons palm sugar
¼ teaspoon citric acid
1 teaspoon finely grated lime zest

In a medium saucepan over medium-high heat, cook the onions in the oil until just beginning to color, about 6 minutes. Add the garlic, carrots, 3 cups of the coconut milk and 1 cup water, and then boil until the carrots are very tender and the mixture is reduced to three-quarters of its original volume.

Transfer to a blender or food processor and purée while still hot until very smooth. Strain through a fine sieve and return to the saucepan, season with salt and keep warm.

In a small saucepan over high heat, combine the remaining 1 cup coconut milk with the lime leaves, lime juice and ginger. Boil until the liquid is reduced by half. Season with salt and strain to remove the solids. Transfer to a blender or food processor and purée on high speed until the mixture foams.

In a small bowl, mix together the dried shrimp, palm sugar, citric acid, and lime zest.

Divide the soup into four warmed soup bowls. Carefully pour the coconut foam over the soup and top with the lime praline. Serve immediately.

WHITE RADISH PURÉE WITH BLACK TRUFFLES

White Hailstone radishes produce a velvety smooth, rich soup. Other mild, spring radishes work well, too, but choose white ones for a clean color. Black winter truffles are a marvel on this soup. Thinly shaved salted radishes tossed in black truffle oil are a fine substitute.

SERVES 4

1 pound Hailstone radishes, trimmed
3 cups heavy cream
1 cup water, or as needed
sea salt

1 tablespoon shaved black truffles
1 tablespoon fresh chervil
2 teaspoons black truffle oil

In a medium saucepan over high heat, combine the radishes, heavy cream, and water. Boil until the radishes are very tender, about 30 minutes.

Transfer to a blender or food processor and purée until very smooth. Strain the radish purée through a fine strainer. Return the radish purée to the saucepan over low heat and thin to desired consistency with the water. Season with salt.

Divide the soup into four warmed soup bowls. Top each with shaved black truffles and chervil. Drizzle with black truffle oil and serve immediately.

- -

WHITE HAILSTONE RADISHES

I originally chose to plant Hailstone white radishes for their unusual, leafy tops. Unlike other radishes, these have smooth, finely textured leaves. While they serve as a nice salad green when small and the radishes make a fine raw snack, it is how they work together in this soup that has made this variety a permanent addition to our farm.

CUCUMBER GAZPACHO
WITH LABNEH & PICKLED VEGETABLES

As the summer turns on the heat and the thought of turning on the stove fills me with dread, I put together this cooling raw soup. The cucumbers are served chilled as a consommé. They add a refreshing coolness that carries the other light ingredients. Labneh, a type of cheese made from strained yogurt, contributes a rich, creamy bite to the soup, while the slivers of pickled young garlic and carrots add a touch of bright acidity. Diced cucumbers round out the dish. This is a two-day recipe—the labneh needs to drain overnight and the cucumber consommé is best chilled overnight.

SERVES 4

1 pound cucumbers, peeled and deseeded, plus ¼ cup peeled, seeded and finely diced cucumbers

2 tablespoons chopped fresh parsley

2 tablespoons chopped fresh mint

¼ cup borage leaves, plus 12 borage flowers for garnish

1 tablespoon sunflower oil

4 ice cubes

sea salt

1 cup plain whole milk yogurt

1 tablespoon very thinly sliced young green garlic (see page 95)

12 tiny carrots, trimmed

½ cup champagne vinegar

2 teaspoons sugar

1 sprig fresh tarragon

extra-virgin olive oil

1 tablespoon ground dried wakame seaweed

In a blender, combine the 1 pound of cucumbers, the parsley, mint, borage leaves, sunflower oil and ice cubes and purée until very smooth. Season with salt.

Line a strainer with cheesecloth and place over a medium bowl. Transfer the cucumber purée to the lined strainer and drain overnight in the refrigerator. Remove the strainer the next day and discard its contents. Set aside the bowl of cucumber consommé.

After puréeing the cucumber mixture and transferring it to a strainer to drain, line a second strainer with cheesecloth and place it over a small bowl. Place the yogurt in the lined strainer and drain it overnight in a refrigerator. The next day, transfer the yogurt cheese in the strainer to a small bowl and season with salt.

In a small heatproof bowl, toss the young garlic and tiny carrots liberally with salt. When they begin to sweat, thoroughly rinse the vegetables and the bowl. Return the vegetables to the bowl.

In a small saucepan over high heat, bring the vinegar, ½ cup water, 1 tablespoon salt, the sugar and tarragon to a boil. Pour the brine over the vegetables. When the brine has cooled, place the vegetables in the refrigerator to pickle overnight. Drain the pickled vegetables before assembling the soup.

To each of four chilled bowls, add a small scoop of yogurt cheese, a few pickled vegetables, and some diced cucumbers. Gently ladle the cucumber consommé into the bowls. Drizzle with olive oil and garnish with the ground seaweed and borage flowers. Serve immediately.

BORAGE

An annual herb grown for its stunning star-shaped violet flowers, borage's flavor is decidedly cucumber. The leaves add a depth of flavor to cucumber-based dishes without the bitterness that often comes along. I like to mix a few finely chopped borage leaves into a salad to add a refreshing quality. The plant's hairy leaves look daunting to work with at first glance, but after a quick blanch in hot water, they are ready to be eaten. Sometimes I'll serve a small salad of the leaves with chilled oysters or mix finely chopped borage in yogurt and serve alongside grilled lamb to great effect.

CHILLED TOMATO SOUP
WITH LOVAGE & JUNIPER

Lovage, a perennial cousin of celery that shares its leaf shape and flavor, imparts a stronger taste so use it sparingly—just a few leaves are enough to provide a wonderful aroma. Celery leaves are a fine substitute, but double their quantity to approximate the flavor. In this soup, I've taken flavor cues from that certain spicy brunch cocktail. The result is elegant and festive.

SERVES 4

6 cups diced tomatoes

3 tablespoons chopped lovage leaves plus 2 tablespoons whole leaves

cayenne pepper

sea salt

2 tablespoons crème fraîche

2 teaspoons freshly grated horseradish

1 tablespoon verjus (see note, page 141)

freshly ground black pepper

12 cherry tomatoes, hollowed

¼ cup sugar, plus more to coat

1 beefsteak or large red heirloom tomato

2 teaspoon red wine vinegar

4 sprigs fresh thyme

4 oven-dried tomatoes, diced (see larder)

2 teaspoons garlic oil (see larder)

1 teaspoon ground juniper berries

Add the diced tomatoes and chopped lovage leaves to a blender or food processor and purée until very smooth. Season with cayenne pepper and salt. Line a strainer with cheesecloth and place over a medium bowl. Pour the tomato purée into the strainer and drain overnight in the refrigerator. Once fully drained, check the tomato consommé for seasoning and adjust if necessary.

In a small bowl, mix the crème fraîche with 1 teaspoon of the horseradish. Season with the verjus, salt and pepper. Place a dollop of the horseradish crème fraîche in each hollowed-out cherry tomato and set aside on a plate.

In a small saucepan, combine the sugar with 1 tablespoon water and bring to a boil. Remove from the heat. When the sugar syrup has cooled to warm, submerge the 2 tablespoons of whole lovage leaves in the saucepan. After a minute, remove the leaves and drain. Coat the leaves in sugar and set aside.

Cut the large tomato into four 1-inch-thick slices, then stamp the slices into ¼-inch rounds with a round cookie cutter, or cut into bite-sized wedges. In a small bowl, combine the rounds or wedges with the vinegar and fresh thyme. Season with salt and pepper, and then marinate for 1 hour.

In four chilled bowls, layer the cherry tomatoes, marinated tomatoes, and oven-dried tomatoes. Gently ladle the tomato consommé into the bowls and lightly drizzle with garlic oil. Garnish with the candied lovage leaves and sprinkle with the ground juniper berries and the remaining teaspoon horseradish. Serve immediately.

BLACK CHICKPEA & SUMMER VEGETABLE RAGOUT

Black chickpeas are similar in flavor and texture to the more common white chickpea but add a striking visual from their jet black color. We grow several hundred pounds of them every year. I especially love their dark black set against the red of tomatoes and the yellow of aioli. Here, I use them in a ragout that catches all the end of the summer vegetables: tomatoes, eggplant, fennel and summer squashes. Feel free to use dried white chickpeas with this recipe if you do not have dried black chickpeas.

SERVES 4

2 cups dried chickpeas

sea salt

1 bay leaf

2 tablespoons olive oil

1 medium onion, julienned

½ cup thinly sliced fennel

1 cup peeled and diced
    eggplant

1 cup diced summer squash

1 tablespoon ras el hanout
    spice mixture

4 cloves garlic, thinly sliced

3 cups diced tomatoes

2 cups tomato juice

1 pinch saffron threads

1 tablespoon warm water

1 cup traditional aïoli
    (see larder)

1 cup chopped summer herbs,
    such as basil, fennel fronds,
    and parsley

In a medium bowl, combine the chickpeas with enough water to cover and soak them overnight. The next day, drain and rinse the soaked chickpeas and transfer to a medium saucepan. Add enough water to cover, season with salt and add the bay leaf. Over medium-high heat, bring the water to a simmer and cook until the chickpeas are tender, about 2 hours, adding water if necessary. Drain the chickpeas and set aside.

In a heavy-bottomed braising pan over medium heat, combine the oil and onion and cook until softened, about 4 minutes. Add the fennel, eggplant, summer squash and ras el hanout and sauté until the vegetables just begin to color, about 6 minutes. Add the garlic and cook until golden, about 4 minutes more. Add the diced tomatoes, tomato juice and chickpeas and bring to a simmer for 10 minutes. Season with salt.

In a small bowl, soften the saffron threads in the warm water for about 5 minutes. Add the aïoli and mix to incorporate.

Divide the vegetables into four warmed soup bowls. Add a dollop of the saffron aïoli and garnish with the fresh summer herbs. Serve immediately.

Overleaf: Black chickpea and summer vegetable ragout and Black chickpeas.

FENNEL PURÉE
WITH TOMATO FONDUTO

Even those who do not love fennel's bright licorice note are captivated by this soup. Cooking transforms the intense licorice flavor to a mellow velvety smoothness. The melted tomato fonduto resonates with flavor while the fennel flower crème adds a floral note.

SERVES 4

3 large fennel bulbs, sliced, plus 2 tablespoons shaved
6 cloves garlic, sliced
1 medium onion, sliced
1 medium potato, peeled and sliced
sea salt
¼ cup heavy cream (optional)
verjus (see page 141)
¼ cup plus 1 tablespoon fennel flowers
2 tablespoons brandy
¼ cup crème fraîche
1 tablespoon chopped fennel fronds
1 teaspoon basic vinaigrette (see larder)
¼ cup tomato fonduto (see larder)

In a large saucepan over medium-high heat, sauté the sliced fennel, garlic and onion until they begin to color. Add the potatoes and water to cover. Bring to a boil over high heat until the water is reduced by three quarters, about 45 minutes. Transfer to a blender and purée until very smooth. Season with salt. Strain through a fine-mesh strainer and return to the saucepan. Thin to the desired consistency with water or the heavy cream. Season again with salt and verjus.

In a saucepan, bring ¼ cup of the fennel flowers and the brandy to a boil, then simmer over low heat for 3 minutes. Cool for 10 minutes; strain into a small bowl. Stir in the crème fraîche and season with salt.

Gently toss the remaining 1 tablespoon fennel flowers, chopped fronds, and bulb shavings with the vinaigrette. Season with salt.

Divide the soup among four soup bowls and add a dollop of the tomato fonduto to each. Top with a little of the crème and garnish with the fennel salad. Serve immediately.

PUMPKIN SOUP WITH DUCK
CONFIT & SPICED PEPITAS

I adore the Japanese varieties of Hokkaido squash like Kabocha and Red Kuri. Deeper in color and flavor than their American cousin, Blue Hubbard, they excel in this soup. The aromatic duck leg confit adds decadence while the pepitas add a playful crunch.

SERVES 4

1 pound Kabocha or Red Kuri squash, halved and deseeded
1 tablespoon sunflower oil
sea salt
2 medium onions, peeled and diced
6 cloves garlic, peeled
1 duck leg confit (see larder)
2 tablespoons pumpkin seeds or pepitas
pinch of chile powder
pinch of ground coriander
2 tablespoons pumpkin seed oil

Preheat the oven to 500°F.

In a roasting pan, lightly coat the squash with oil and season with salt. Roast in the oven until the squash starts to color and is very tender, about 15 minutes. Let the squash cool, then peel.

In a medium saucepan over medium-high heat, place the squash, onions, and garlic and add enough water to cover. Boil until the water is reduced to three-quarters, about 45 minutes. Transfer to a blender while still hot and purée until very smooth. Season with salt.

In a small sauté pan over medium heat, warm the duck confit. Remove the leg from the pan, pull the meat from the bone, and shred into small pieces. Place the shredded meat in a small bowl and season with salt, if needed.

In a small sauté pan over medium heat, toast the pumpkin seeds with the chile powder and ground coriander until fragrant.

Divide the soup into four warmed soup bowls. Top each with the shredded duck and spiced pumpkin seeds. Drizzle the soup with the pumpkin seed oil and serve immediately.

DUCK-DUCK-GOOSE
DUCK CONSOMMÉ, DUCK PROSCIUTTO & GOOSE SPÄTZLE

Classic duck soup left in the hands of an often irreverent chef sometimes yields a dish like this. The lighthearted name belies the technique behind the soup, which includes starting the consommé a day ahead. We raise Tolouse geese on the farm and I admire their wonderful flavor.

SERVES 4

3 pounds duck bones

12 black peppercorns plus 1 tablespoon black peppercorns

2 carrots, sliced, plus 1 carrot, minced

4 ribs celery, sliced, plus 2 celery ribs, minced

1 large onion, sliced, plus 1 medium onion, minced

2 tablespoons sunflower oil

1 leek, julienned

2 tablespoons duck fat

8 egg whites

1 cup parsley stems plus 1 tablespoon minced fresh parsley leaves

2 tablespoons chopped fresh orange peel

2 pieces star anise

2 cardamom pods

sea salt

1 cup all-purpose flour

¾ cup whole milk

1 large egg

½ smoked goose breast, minced, preferably Schlitz's

3 ounces duck prosciutto, finely julienned (see larder)

2 tablespoons chopped fall herb leaves, such as fennel fronds, chervil, parsley and thyme

Preheat the oven to 500°F.

Place the duck bones in a roasting pan and roast until mahogany in color, 30 to 45 minutes. Transfer to a stockpot and add 1½ gallons water and the 12 peppercorns. Bring to a full boil over high heat for 7 minutes. Reduce to a low simmer for 2 hours, skimming the surface to remove fat and other impurities.

Meanwhile, in a large sauté pan over high heat, sauté the sliced carrots, celery, and onion in the oil until they begin to color. Add to the stock for the last 40 minutes of simmering. Strain the stock to discard any solids and chill overnight.

In a large sauté pan over medium-high heat, sauté the minced onion, carrot, celery and leeks in the duck fat until they begin to color. Transfer to a container and chill overnight.

The next day, mix the vegetables with the egg whites, parsley stems, orange peels, star anise, cardamom, and 1 tablespoon black peppercorns. Place the duck stock in a stockpot and whisk the vegetable mixture into the very cold stock.

Place the stockpot over medium-high heat and stir once or twice to prevent the vegetables from sticking to the bottom. When the stock has reached 140°F, the egg whites will begin to coagulate and capture impurities in the stock. Continue to heat until the egg whites have completely solidified, about 10 minutes more. Remove from the heat and let the stock stand for 10 minutes.

Very gently, with the back of a ladle, push down on the egg and vegetable raft. Use the same ladle to transfer the stock into a strainer lined with cheesecloth that is positioned over a large bowl. Transfer the strained consommé to a clean stockpot and bring to a simmer over medium heat. Skim off any foam that has formed, season with salt and set aside over low heat.

In the bowl of a stand mixer, combine the flour, milk, egg, goose meat, minced parsley and salt to taste. Mix on medium for 4 minutes, until the batter becomes elastic. Working in batches over boiling salted water, pass the spätzle batter through a coarse colander or food mill so that small pea-sized droplets fall into the boiling water. Cook until the dumplings are al dente, about 4 minutes. Use a handheld strainer to transfer the spätzle to a sheet tray to cool. Continue cooking until all the dumplings are done.

Divide the spätzle among four warmed bowls. Gently ladle the duck consommé into the bowls and top with the julienned duck prosciutto. Garnish with the herbs and serve immediately.

SUNCHOKE SOUP
WITH LOCAL MUSHROOMS & SUNFLOWER SEED GRANOLA

Sunchokes, or Jerusalem artichokes, are the edible, potato-like tuber that grows beneath one of several varieties of common sunflower. Native to the western United States, it is no surprise they are a staple at our farm and restaurant. They possess a flavor somewhat like a potato crossed with the nuttiness of almonds. Here, I've played off of those flavors by pairing a quick sauté of mushrooms from a local farm. To add a playful crunch to this otherwise serious soup, I've topped it with a granola made from popped grains and toasted sunflower seeds.

SERVES 4

1 pound sunchokes, sliced

1 medium onion, thinly sliced, plus ½ cup finely diced onions

6 cloves garlic, thinly sliced

½ cup thinly sliced fennel bulb

2 tablespoons plus ¼ cup sunflower oil

chicken or vegetable stock (optional, see larder)

1 cup heavy cream (optional)

sea salt

sherry vinegar to taste

2 tablespoon unsalted butter, softened

2 cups sliced fresh shiitake, crimini or oyster mushrooms

freshly ground black pepper

3 tablespoons quinoa

2 tablespoons amaranth seeds

2 tablespoons toasted sunflower seeds

1 teaspoon dried lovage or celery leaves

In a medium saucepan over high heat, bring salted water to a boil. Blanch the sunchokes until just tender, about 4 minutes, then strain.

In a large saucepan over medium-high heat, sauté the sunchokes, sliced onion, garlic, and fennel in 2 tablespoons oil until they begin to color, about 6 minutes. Add enough water, chicken or vegetable stock to cover and bring to a boil over high heat until the liquid reduces to three-quarters of the original volume, about 45 minutes.

Transfer to a blender and purée until very smooth. Strain through a fine-mesh strainer and return to the saucepan. Thin the soup to the desired consistency with water or the heavy cream. Season with salt and sherry vinegar.

Add the butter and diced onions to a sauté pan over medium heat and sauté until the onions begin to color. Stir in the mushrooms and sauté until browned. Season with salt and pepper.

Add the remaining ¼ cup oil to a small saucepan over medium-high heat. When the oil has reached 350°F, add the quinoa and amaranth seeds. Stir occasionally until the grains start popping. Once they've popped, transfer to a fine-mesh strainer to drain the oil. Place the popped grains on paper towels and blot any remaining oil. Let cool, then transfer to a small bowl with the sunflower seeds. Season with salt and pepper and toss the granola well.

Divide the soup into four warmed bowls. Top each with the mushroom mixture. Sprinkle with the granola and dried lovage leaves. Serve immediately.

SMOKED HERITAGE TURKEY, WILD RICE & FENNEL SOUP

More so than most soups, this showcases our farm's abundance even on the cusp of winter. At Thanksgiving time, we harvest our spectacular Red Bourbon turkeys for the big dinner. Already rich in taste, once smoked, our turkeys explode with flavor. The results are put to good use in this comforting yet elegant soup. Wild rice adds a toothsome bite and fennel a haunting sweetness and depth. I often wish for a second Thanksgiving each winter just for an excuse to make this soup again.

SERVES 4

2 pounds smoked turkey
   bones
2 smoked turkey legs
5 tablespoons sunflower oil
4 medium onions, diced
6 cloves garlic, diced
1 large carrot, diced
2 ribs celery, diced
1 cup wild rice
sea salt
2 large fennel bulbs, diced,
   plus 1 tablespoon chopped
   fennel fronds
3 cups peeled and diced
   winter squash
1 tablespoon minced fresh
   sage leaves

Place the turkey bones and legs in a stockpot. Add enough water to cover and bring to a full boil over high heat for 7 minutes. Reduce the heat to low and simmer for 2 hours, skimming the surface of the stock to remove impurities.

While the stock is simmering, combine 2 tablespoons of the oil, half of the diced onions, the garlic, carrots and celery in a large sauté pan over high heat and sauté until the vegetables begin to color. Transfer to the stock for the last 40 minutes of simmering.

Transfer the smoked turkey legs to a cutting board to cool. Strain the stock, discarding the solids. Return the stock to the cleaned stockpot over low heat. Remove the meat from the smoked turkey legs, dice and set aside.

Place the wild rice in a medium saucepan. Add enough salted water to cover and bring to a boil over high heat. Reduce to a simmer, cover and cook until the rice kernels puff open, 40 to 45 minutes. Uncover, fluff the rice with a fork, and simmer for another 5 minutes. Drain off any excess water and set the rice aside.

In a large sauté pan over medium heat, combine 2 tablespoons of the oil, the remaining diced onions and the diced fennel. Cook until the vegetables begin to color, about 7 minutes. Season with salt, transfer to a plate and set aside.

Return the sauté pan to the stove over medium-high heat and lightly coat with the remaining 1 tablespoon oil. Add the winter squash and sauté until it begins to color, about 7 minutes. Remove from the heat, toss with the sage and season with salt.

Add the smoked turkey meat, wild rice, fennel and squash to the simmering stockpot and mix well. Over medium heat, bring to a boil, then reduce to a low simmer for 10 minutes. Season with salt.

Divide the soup into four warmed bowls. Garnish with the fennel fronds and serve immediately.

CHRYSANTHEMUM

Chrysanthemum leaves add an enigmatic herbal note that lifts this whole recipe. Available in Asian specialty markets, cilantro or shiso are fine substitutes.

BURDOCK ROOT VELOUTÉ
WITH PICKLED SHIITAKES & CHRYSANTHEMUM LEAVES

While reading an old Japanese cookbook, I came across a reference to burdock root as a winter "tonic" to restore the body. It struck a chord as I knew burdock's long slender roots store minerals from deep in the soil. I got to work crafting a dish that carried the spirit of that idea. This soup balances burdock's earthiness with the perfume of toasted sesame seeds and the tang of pickled shiitakes.

SERVES 4

1 cup julienned fresh shiitake
   mushrooms
1 tablespoon ground dried
   wakame seaweed
3 tablespoon rice vinegar
sea salt
1 tablespoon sunflower oil
1 large onion, diced
10 cloves garlic, diced
1 large potato, diced
1 pound burdock roots, peeled
   and diced
1 tablespoon fresh or pickled
   chrysanthemum leaves,
   chopped (see note, above)
2 tablespoons sesame seeds,
   toasted

Place the mushrooms in a small heatproof bowl. In a small saucepan over high heat, combine the wakame seaweed with the rice vinegar and season with salt. Bring to a boil, then pour over the mushrooms and let sit in the brine for 1 hour.

Meanwhile, in a large saucepan over medium-high heat, combine the oil, onion, garlic, potato and burdock root. Cook until the garlic begins to brown, then add enough water to cover. Boil until the soup is reduced to three-quarters of its original volume.

While still hot, transfer the soup to a blender and purée until very smooth. Return to the saucepan and thin to desired consistency with water. Season with salt and keep warm over low heat.

Divide the soup into four warmed bowls. Top with the pickled mushrooms, chrysanthemum leaves and toasted sesame seeds. Serve immediately.

SALADS

REGARDLESS OF THE SEASON, SALADS CELEBRATE THE BOUNTY OF THE FARM.
I LET THE INGREDIENTS SHINE, WHETHER THROUGH TENDER LETTUCES AND
GREENS OR VIVIDLY FLAVORED CRUNCHY VEGETABLES. NO HEAVY DRESSINGS
HERE. INSTEAD, I OPT FOR A SIMPLE, LIGHT VINAIGRETTE THAT HIGHLIGHTS THE
INGREDIENTS' NATURAL FLAVORS. I OFTEN COMBINE RAW AND COOKED ELEMENTS
IN A SALAD TO ADD SAVORY DEPTH AND INTEREST.

SPINACH SALAD
WITH GOAT CHEESE FRITES

Early season spinach is especially sweet when the nights are cold and the last of the snow is still melting. Bright, fresh goat cheese, cooked here as if it were a little surprise package, lifts the fresh spinach.

SERVES 4

12 medium shallots, peeled
2 teaspoons sunflower oil
sea salt
2 tablespoons quinoa flour
½ cup rice flour
½ cup plus 2 tablespoons soda water

1½ cups goat cheese
¼ cup garlic oil (see larder)
1 tablespoon red wine vinegar
1 sprig fresh thyme
2 tablespoons hazelnuts, toasted
½ pound spinach

Preheat the oven to 450°F.

On a baking sheet, dress the shallots in the sunflower oil and season with salt. Roast until the shallots are beginning to brown and are very tender, about 15 minutes. Let cool then chop the shallots.

In a medium saucepan over medium-high heat, heat 2 inches of oil to 375°F.

Combine the flours in a medium bowl and mix in 1 teaspoon salt and the soda water until smooth; it should be as thick as pancake batter.

Form the goat cheese into 12 balls and dip into the batter one at a time, coating them completely. Using a fork and working in batches, fry the balls in the oil until golden, 30 to 60 seconds. Drain on paper towels.

In a small saucepan over low heat, heat the garlic oil, vinegar, thyme and hazelnuts until fragrant, about 6 minutes. Season with salt and whisk well.

Toss the spinach and roasted shallots with the warm vinaigrette. Season with salt and toss again. Divide among four salad plates. Top with the crispy goat cheese and serve immediately.

PEA TENDRILS
WITH WARM POACHED CHICKEN

Here, I've combined warm, moist poached chicken with the bright flavors of the farm's first harvests each spring. The crunchy radishes add zip to the warm salad, while the grilled spring onions pull all the elements together.

SERVES 4

4 spring onion tops
1 tablespoon sunflower oil
sea salt and freshly ground black pepper
2 cups assorted baby radishes, trimmed and thinly shaved

¼ cup whole-grain mustard vinaigrette (see larder)
3 cups poached chicken, sliced (see larder)
2 cups pea tendrils and flowers (see note, opposite)

In a small bowl, dress the onions in the oil and season with salt and pepper. Grill over a charcoal or wood flame until lightly charred, about 4 minutes. Alternatively, char the onions over a stovetop gas flame. Cut into 2-inch lengths. Transfer to a medium bowl and toss with the radishes and half of the vinaigrette. Season with salt.

In a small saucepan over medium heat, heat the chicken until warmed through, about 6 minutes.

Divide the radish salad among four salad plates. Top with the chicken, garnish with the pea tendrils and flowers and lightly dress with the remaining vinaigrette. Serve immediately.

PEA TENDRILS

Edible, delicious and delicate, pea tendrils are the soft leaves and curly tips at the ends of pea plants. At the restaurant, they provide a vivid pea flavor a month or more before the earliest of the pea harvests. Best from your garden, they are also available at your local farmer's market and specialty stores early in the spring. Avoid the temptation of using them late in the season, as they often turn tough.

PARSLEY SALAD
WITH BEEF CARPACCIO & FAVAS

This is an assertive salad in which fresh flat-leaf parsley takes the place of traditional lettuces. Paired with warm roasted onions and peppery beef, the parsley comes into its own. Fall-planted parsley often survives our harsh winters. Its first leaves each spring are a treasure. I always use fresh fava beans here.

SERVES 4

8 ounces beef tenderloin
salt and freshly ground
   black pepper
1 tablespoon garlic oil
   (see larder)
1 cup shelled fava beans
¼ cup basic vinaigrette
   (see larder)

1 cup julienned balsamic
   roasted onions
   (see larder)
3 cups fresh flat-leaf
   parsley leaves
½ cup thinly sliced asiago
   cheese

Season the beef liberally with salt and pepper and dress with the garlic oil. Grill over a hot charcoal or wood fire until lightly charred on the outside but still raw on the inside. Transfer to the freezer to chill until almost frozen; the beef should have a slushy texture. As thinly as possible, slice the beef and set aside in the refrigerator.

In a medium saucepan over high heat, blanch the favas in boiling salted water until their color brightens, about 2 minutes. Remove from the water and set aside to cool. When cool enough to handle, remove the beans from their jackets by tearing one edge then firmly squeezing the bean.

In a medium bowl, dress the favas with the vinaigrette. Add the roasted onions and parsley. Season with salt and toss well.

Lay out the slices of the beef on the bottoms of four salad plates. Top with the parsley salad and garnish with the cheese. Serve immediately.

SUMMER PANZANELLA

Panzanella is a traditional Italian salad using grilled bread and olive oil as a starting point. From there, I'll often let the farm steer the direction. If the tomatoes look great, in they go. Beautiful eggplant or summer squash, why not? Treating basil and parsley as if they were lettuce is a bit unconventional, but I love the occasional burst of flavor they provide to this robust salad.

SERVES 4

4 slices fresh sourdough
   bread
1 medium summer
   squash, thinly sliced
2 tablespoons olive oil
sea salt
1 cup fresh parsley leaves
1 cup fresh basil leaves
½ cup fresh mint leaves
2 cups mixed lettuces
½ cup diced heirloom
   tomatoes

½ cup diced cucumbers
½ cup balsamic roasted
   onions, chopped
   (see larder)
½ teaspoon minced garlic
3 tablespoons basic
   vinaigrette (see larder)
1 tablespoon balsamic
   vinegar
¼ cup shaved Parmesan
   cheese

Dress the bread slices and summer squash in the olive oil and season with salt. Grill over a wood or charcoal fire until golden, about 3 minutes, or toast in the oven for 10 minutes. Cut the bread and squash into rough chunks and transfer to a large bowl.

Add the herbs, lettuces, tomatoes, cucumbers, roasted onions, garlic and vinaigrette and toss well. Season with salt and toss again.

Divide the salad among four plates. Top with the vinegar and cheese. Serve immediately.

HEIRLOOM TOMATO SALAD

No farm to table restaurant worth its salt can go through a summer without a version of the now classic heirloom tomato salad. Never wanting to be numbed to the beauty of summer tomatoes, I strive to balance our version of fresh, vine-ripened tomatoes with other tomato textures and flavors, like roasted or dried. In the end this yields a salad that bursts with fresh tomato ripeness but continues to captivate all summer long.

SERVES 4

6 heirloom plum tomatoes, quartered

2 tablespoons sunflower oil

sea salt and freshly ground black pepper

4 oven-dried tomato halves (see larder)

4 thin slices pecorino Romano cheese

1 teaspoon capers, plus 1 teaspoon caper brine

4 ounces puff pastry dough, rolled thinly and cut into 2-inch squares

¼ cup grated Parmesan cheese

1 tablespoon tomato powder (see larder)

1 large tomato, such as beefsteak or Brandywine, quartered

1 cup plus 1 tablespoon olive oil

4 sprigs fresh thyme

2 bay leaves

2 cups sliced or quartered heirloom tomatoes, various types

1 tablespoon minced fresh marjoram

1 tablespoon julienned fresh mint

1 tablespoon red wine vinegar

1 cup basil coulis (see larder)

Preheat the oven to 425°F.

In a small bowl, combine the plum tomatoes with 1 tablespoon of sunflower oil. Season with salt and pepper and toss well. Spread onto a baking sheet in a single layer and bake until the tomatoes begin to brown and have dried somewhat, about 15 minutes. Set aside to let cool.

Place the oven-dried tomatoes on a second baking sheet. Top each with the pecorino, capers, brine, the remaining 1 tablespoon sunflower oil and pastry dough. Bake until the pastry is golden, about 8 minutes. Remove the tarts from the oven and set aside.

On a silicone baking mat, form 12 small piles of Parmesan. Top each with the tomato powder. Bake in the oven until the cheese is golden. Set aside to let cool; the cheese will crisp up as it cools, becoming a cracker.

Season the beefsteak tomatoes with salt. Place in a small pot with 1 cup of the olive oil, the thyme and bay leaves. Poach over very low heat, until softened, about 25 minutes. Remove the pan from the heat and let stand for 20 minutes. Drain the tomatoes from the oil and set aside.

In a small bowl, combine the sliced heirloom tomatoes, herbs, vinegar and remaining 1 tablespoon olive oil. Season with salt and toss well.

HEIRLOOM TOMATOES

There are more tomato varieties than days in a lifetime it seems. For this salad, I combine a variety of tomato sizes, colors and flavors. From large reds like beefsteak or Jet Star to plums like San Marzano to small yellows like sungolds, I love them all. But for the deepest, richest flavor I prefer the black varieties like Black Prince, Black Krim and Principe Borghese. These are low-acid varieties with great flavor raw and even better flavor roasted. Choosing the best varieties for one's garden requires some experimentation. Every garden is different as is every palate. Fortunately, there are enough varieties out there for everyone to have a favorite.

WITH TOMATO FARCI & TOMATO PARFAIT

TOMATO FARCI

3 tablespoons tapenade
  (see larder)

3 tablespoons diced grilled
  summer squash (see note,
  page 78)

1 tablespoon basic vinaigrette
  (see larder)

4 Principe Borghese tomatoes,
  tops removed and hollowed

TOMATO PARFAIT

¼ cup heavy cream

2 tablespoons Parmesan
  cheese

½ cup tomato fonduto
  (see larder)

sea salt

12 cherry tomatoes, hollowed

To make the farci, in a small bowl, combine the tapenade, summer squash and vinaigrette. Toss well and fill each tomato with the tapenade mixture.

To make the parfait, in a small bowl, combine the cream, cheese, and tomato fonduto. Season with salt and fill the cherry tomatoes with the cream mixture.

Divide the marinated tomatoes and herbs between four plates. Garnish with the roasted tomatoes, tomato tarts, frico, poached tomatoes, farci, parfait and basil coulis. Serve immediately.

Overleaf: Haricots verts and Haricots verts with potatoes & summer truffles

HARICOTS VERTS WITH POTATOES & SUMMER TRUFFLES

Each summer, as our lettuce wilts under the intense temperatures, I look for cool salad alternatives to beat the heat. A perennial favorite combines chilled baby green beans, olive oil–poached potatoes and goat cheese. When your supply of summer truffles runs low, white truffle oil makes a fine substitute.

SERVES 4

2 cups fingerling potatoes
sea salt
1 sprig fresh rosemary
5 cloves garlic
1½ cups olive oil
3 cups haricots verts
2 cups tatsoi leaves
2 tablespoons finely
   julienned lemon zest

3 tablespoons basic
   vinaigrette (see larder)
6 squash blossoms,
   julienned
6 ounces fresh or aged
   chèvre
1 tablespoon shaved
   summer truffles
   (optional)

In a medium saucepan over high heat, blanch the potatoes in heavily salted boiling water for 5 minutes. Strain through a colander and then return to the pan. Add the rosemary and garlic and enough olive oil to cover the potatoes. Place over low heat and cook slowly until the potaotes are tender, about 30 minutes.

In a large pot over high heat, blanch the haricots verts in boiling salted water until their color brightens, about 30 seconds. Immediately transfer the beans into ice water to halt the cooking and cool fully. Drain and transfer to a large bowl. Add the potatoes, tatsoi, lemon zest and vinaigrette. Season with salt and toss.

Divide among four chilled plates. Top with the squash blossoms, cheese and truffles, if using. Serve immediately.

TATSOI

Tatsoi, a miniature version of bok choy, comes into its own in the heat of the summer. It thrives in scorching sun, yielding succulent, juicy leaves. Throughout the summer, I plant tatsoi in rapid succession, about every ten days. The young, tender leaves are great in salads like this one. Larger leaves can be used in a quick sauté. I leave my last crop growing in the fields until the dead of winter, as this plant is one of the most cold-hearty as well.

TOM THUMB LETTUCE
WITH GRILLED APPLES & CHEDDAR

Of the many types of butter lettuce, my favorite is Tom Thumb. It balances tender leaves with just enough texture to add interest to a salad. And its diminutive size is so cute on the plate! Tom Thumb's buttery leaves are a perfect foil for the toothsome cheddar, apple and pecan elements.

SERVES 4

2 Honeycrisp apples, cut into ¼-inch slices

2 tablespoons plus ¼ cup sunflower oil

sea salt

1 cup chopped toasted pecans, plus ½ cup whole for garnish

¼ cup roasted garlic cloves (see larder)

lemon juice to taste

½ pound Tom Thumb lettuce

3 tablespoons basic vinaigrette (see larder)

1 cup sliced Cheddar cheese

In a small bowl, dress the apple slices in 2 tablespoons of the oil and season with salt. Grill over a wood or charcoal fire until lightly charred, about 2 minutes, or broil in the oven. Set aside.

In a blender, purée the chopped pecans and roasted garlic with ¼ cup water until very smooth. With the motor running, slowly add the remaining ¼ cup oil and purée until fully incorporated. Season with salt and lemon juice.

Put the lettuce, vinaigrette, cheese and whole pecans in a large bowl. Season with salt and toss.

Divide the salad among four salad plates and top with the grilled apples. Drizzle the tops of the salads with the pecan purée and serve immediately.

ARUGULA WITH PICKLED
DATES & FOURME D'AMBERT

Cool nights and gently warm days are the ideal for arugula. In summer, arugula protests the hot days by turning from pleasantly peppery to a fiery inferno. As the nights turn chilly, I return again to the rich nuttiness of arugula. Here, I've paired it with robust sweet, salty, sour and bitter flavors.

SERVES 4

1 cup dates, cut into strips

¾ cup red wine vinegar

2 cardamom pods

2 fresh bay leaves

sea salt

1 lemon

1 tablespoon sunflower oil

½ pound arugula

3 tablespoons basic vinaigrette (see larder)

6 ounces Fourme d'Ambert cheese, crumbled

In a small saucepan over high heat, combine the dates, vinegar, cardamom and bay leaves with ¼ cup water. Cook until the dates soften, about 6 minutes. Remove from the heat, season with salt and set aside.

Slice the lemon paper-thin on a mandolin or with a sharp knife. Combine the lemon slices and oil in a small bowl. Season with salt and toss well. Grill the lemon on a wood or charcoal fire until lightly charred, about 2 minutes.

In a large bowl, dress the arugula with the vinaigrette. Season with salt and toss again.

Divide the arugula among four salad plates. Garnish with the cheese, grilled lemons and dates. Serve immediately.

JILL'S FALL KITCHEN GARDEN SALAD

This salad, with its cascade of delicate textures and bursts of flavor, is simple to make for those who garden but daunting for those who don't. Its simple beauty, or difficulty, lies in the accessibility of the ingredients. For those with a kitchen garden, it requires only a quick harvest and a gentle touch. For those without a garden, I have no advice other than a trip to your local farmer's market. The ease of creating memorable food, as demonstrated by this salad, convinced me to start the farm.

SERVES 4

12 baby carrots, trimmed
sunflower oil
sea salt
1 tablespoon handmade
  vinegar (see larder)
1 teaspoon minced shallot
1 sprig fresh thyme
¼ pound baby lettuces
1 cup baby Swiss chard

1 cup baby kale
1 cup fresh chervil
1 tablespoon fresh burnet
  leaves
2 tablespoons chopped
  leek roots
1 tablespoon chives, cut
  into 1-inch lengths

Preheat the oven to 450°F.

In a small bowl, combine the carrots with 2 teaspoons sunflower oil and season with salt. Transfer to a baking sheet and roast until golden, about 8 minutes. Set aside to cool.

In a small bowl, whisk together 5 tablespoons sunflower oil with the vinegar, shallot, thyme and a pinch of salt.

In a large bowl, combine the roasted carrots, baby lettuces, Swiss chard, kale and herbs. Dress lightly with the vinaigrette and serve immediately.

ESCAROLE WITH YOGURT, POMEGRANATE & PISTACHIO

One of the heartiest greens we grow, escarole comes into its own deep into the fall and in early winter. After the first frosts, the strong bitterness of escarole and other endives falls away as the leaves pick up a rich sweetness. This balance of robust flavor and sweetness along with escarole's ability to stand up to cold nights makes it a great fit for salads in November and December. Here, I add festive accompaniments like creamy handmade yogurt, tart pomegranate and toasted pistachios.

SERVES 4

½ cup Greek yogurt
1 tablespoon garlic oil
  (see larder)
2 teaspoons honey
a pinch of ground
  cardamom
sea salt

½ pound escarole
½ cup pomegranate
  seeds
¼ cup pistachios, toasted
  and chopped
3 tablespoons basic
  vinaigrette (see larder)

In a small bowl, combine the yogurt, oil, honey and cardamom. Season with salt and mix well.

In a large bowl, combine the escarole, pomegranate, pistachios and vinaigrette. Season with salt and toss well.

Divide the escarole mixture among four salad plates. Drizzle with the yogurt sauce and serve immediately.

SALT-ROASTED BEET SALAD
WITH STILTON BREAD PUDDING & SHALLOT CONFIT

What is it about beets buried in salt that makes the flavor resonate? Why aren't they too salty? I don't know why. But I do know they are delicious and foolproof. I learned this cooking technique while on a trip to France, and I was incredulous when it was explained to me. My French was very rusty, but I remembered the directions and my friend kept repeating, "Really! It works. Believe me!" So that's my advice to you, too.

SERVES 4

2 large beets

sea salt

5 tablespoons basic
vinaigrette (see larder)

¼ cup roasted garlic
(see larder)

1 medium onion, julienned

1 tablespoon sunflower oil

2 cups cubed sourdough
bread

½ cup heavy cream

1 cup whole milk

1 large egg

½ cup Stilton blue cheese,
crumbled

freshly ground black pepper

2 bay leaves

8 peppercorns

8 shallots, julienned

¾ cup white wine

2 heads Belgian endives,
leaves separated

Preheat the oven to 400°F and grease a baking dish.

Place the beets in a heavy roasting pan and cover with 3 to 4 cups salt. Roast until a knife pierces the beets easily, about 45 minutes. Transfer to a colander and rinse in cool water. Peel the beets and rinse lightly again. Thinly slice, place in a bowl and dress with 2 tablespoons of the vinaigrette. Set aside.

In a small sauté pan over medium heat, combine the garlic, onion and oil. Cook until the onion just begins to color, about 6 minutes. Transfer to a large bowl and add the bread, cream, milk, egg and cheese. Season with salt and pepper and mix well. Transfer to the prepared baking dish and smooth the top. Bake until the bread pudding is set, about 30 minutes. Set aside in a warm place.

Place the bay leaves and peppercorns on a 7-inch piece of cheesecloth. Tie the ends together, forming a sachet. Place it in a small saucepan along with the shallots and wine and boil over high heat until fully reduced. Season with salt.

In a large bowl, combine the endives with the remaining 3 tablespoons vinaigrette. Season with salt. Divide among four salad plates and top with the beets, slices of bread pudding and shallots. Serve immediately.

WINTER ROOTS ROASTED IN EMBERS

This warm salad says "winter" to me. It is what I want to eat as the nights turn very cold. At the restaurant, we smoke various ingredients in plum or apple wood. Here, I roast large winter root vegetables in the wood's smoking embers. While still warm, the roots are tossed with sweet winter spinach, crisp sage and Parmesan. It always amazes me when I'm able to make a salad as alive as this in the dead of winter.

SERVES 4

fruit wood, preferably plum
   (see note)
1½ cups finely grated
   Parmesan cheese
2 large heirloom carrots,
   trimmed
2 parsnips, trimmed
4 sunchokes, trimmed
4 parsley roots, trimmed
2 salsify roots, trimmed
¼ cup sunflower oil
1 cup fresh sage leaves
½ pound large-leafed spinach
2 tablespoons basic
   vinaigrette (see larder)
sea salt

Preheat the oven to 400°F. In a grill, start a wood or charcoal fire. When the fire is burning steadily, add pieces of plum wood.

Spread the Parmesan on a nonstick baking mat set on a baking sheet. Bake until golden, about 5 minutes. Remove from the oven and set aside to cool. The cheese will crisp up as it cools.

Place the root vegetables directly on and alongside the coals of the fire, placing thicker roots on the coals and thinner ones alongside. Roast until tender, 10 to 15 minutes. Remove the roots and wipe away any ash with a damp towel. Trim away any burnt parts and cut into bite-sized pieces.

Heat the oil in a small saucepan over medium-high heat. Fry the sage briefly until crisp, about 1 minute. Transfer to paper towels to drain.

In a large bowl, combine the spinach, warm roots, sage, baked Parmesan, or frico, and vinaigrette. Season with salt and toss well. Divide the salad among four salad plates and serve immediately.

FRUIT WOODS

I'm lucky to employ a professional fruit forager, Colin, for the restaurant. In the summer, he surprises us with freshly harvested fruits and berries from trees and bushes across the countryside. Many times I've asked him where he found a particular harvest, but Colin keeps his cards close to his vest and I doubt he'll ever tell me. Each winter, he prunes his hidden trees and shows up at the restaurant with a truckload of meticulously trimmed branches, ready to go into our large smoker. Fruit woods are best for smoking as they lend a wonderful perfume that is never harsh or bitter. I find plum wood the most aromatic. If you don't have a secretive fruit forager as a friend, I suggest ordering the wood online. Roasting the winter roots in the oven is also possible and even delicious. Searching for the wood is worth it, though.

WARM MARINATED BEETS
WITH POPPED WILD RICE

This lively, fun take on the classic beet salad is perfect for erasing the wintertime blues. With great variations in textures, flavors and colors provided by the red grapefruit, popped rice and avocado, it always uplifts the spirit.

SERVES 4

3 large beets plus 1 cup
   beet leaves
sea salt
3 tablespoons basic
   vinaigrette (see larder)
1 red grapefruit
2 tablespoons agave
1 tablespoon sunflower oil,
   plus more for popping
¼ cup wild rice
1 large onion, sliced into rings
1 avocado, peeled, pitted and
   cut into chunks
¼ cup chopped toasted
   almonds

Preheat the oven to 400°F.

Place the beets in a heavy roasting pan and cover with 3 to 4 cups salt. Roast until a knife pierces the beets easily, about 45 minutes. Transfer to a colander and rinse in cool water. Peel the beets and rinse lightly again. Cut into wedges, place in a bowl and dress with 2 tablespoons of the vinaigrette.

Remove 1 tablespoon zest from the grapefruit. Peel and segment; squeeze 2 tablespoons juice and reserve the juice and remaining segments. In a small saucepan over high heat, combine the zest with enough water to cover. Bring to a boil for 1 minute. Discard the water and return the zest to the pan with fresh water to cover. Repeat the process until the zest is no longer bitter; this usually takes four times. After draining the final time, combine the zest with the agave and grapefruit juice in the saucepan and boil until reduced by half. Set aside.

In a medium saucepan over high heat, heat the oil until shimmery. Add the wild rice and cook, stirring constantly, until it pops, 2 to 3 minutes. Transfer to paper towels to drain.

Over a wood or charcoal fire, or in a grill pan, over high heat, grill the onion rings until lightly charred on both sides. Transfer to a medium bowl. Add the remaining vinaigrette, beet leaves, season with salt and toss.

Divide the salad among four salad plates. Garnish with the roasted beets, avocado, almonds, candied zest and popped rice. Serve immediately.

APPETIZERS

UNLIKE OTHER COURSES THAT NEED TO ACCOMPLISH A LOT, APPETIZERS ARE SMALLER, DIRECT DISHES THAT ARE IDEAL FOR SHOWCASING THE FLAVORS THAT INSPIRE US: PEAS THAT EXPLODE WITH SWEET FLAVOR, THE VIVID AROMA OF BASIL, FRESH CORN JUST MINUTES FROM ITS HARVEST. COOKING TECHNIQUES ASIDE, THESE DISHES ARE QUITE SIMPLE: AN INSPIRATION FROM THE FIELD COMBINED WITH THE QUEST FOR THE PERFECT BITE.

CARROT & CHEVRE TERRINE
WITH LAVENDER ALMONDS

Thinning the long rows of carrots every year yields baskets full of undersized baby carrots. What to do with them was a problem until I came up with this dish where they shine. The technique of the terrine is a simple layering of cooked baby carrots and fresh goat cheese. Once chilled, the goat cheese firms up and the terrine holds its shape. I've taken a cue from herbes de Provence for the accompaniments; the fresh herbs and delicate lavender scent make this a special dish.

SERVES 6 TO 8

2 cups baby carrots, trimmed
sunflower oil
2 cups fresh goat cheese
2 tablespoons minced fresh
  chervil
1 tablespoon minced fresh
  parsley
1 tablespoon minced fresh
  tarragon
2 teaspoons freshly ground
  black pepper
1 tablespoon fresh lavender
½ cup sugar
1 cup whole almonds
unsalted butter

Cut the carrots into quarters lengthwise. In a medium saucepan over high heat, blanch the carrots in salted boiling water until very tender, about 10 minutes. Drain the carrots through a colander and cool completely under running water or in an ice bath.

Coat the inside of a 2-inch terrine mold lightly with oil. Line the mold with plastic wrap allowing several inches of plastic to overhang on all sides. Lightly sprinkle 2 tablespoons of the goat cheese in a layer in the bottom of the mold. Add a quarter of the carrots on top. Press the carrots and cheese firmly to push out any air and to even the layer up. Repeat with more cheese and carrots until they are used up.

Fold the overhanging plastic back over the terrine. Press very firmly on the wrapped terrine to expel any trapped air. Chill for 2 hours in the refrigerator.

On a clean work surface, lay out a clean piece of plastic wrap large enough to fully wrap the terrine. Mix the herbs and pepper in a small bowl. Spread one quarter of the mixture out on top of the plastic in a rectangle equal to the size of the terrine. Unwrap the terrine and place it on top of the herbs. Gently press the remaining herbs onto the sides of the terrine. Wrap the terrine in the plastic and return it to the refrigerator.

Preheat the oven to 350°F.

Place a 7-inch piece of cheesecloth on a clean work surface. Put the lavender in the center, draw up the sides and tie to make a bundle or sachet.

In a small saucepan over high heat, bring ¼ cup water along with the sugar and lavender to a boil. Add the almonds and simmer for 10 minutes. Remove the pan from the heat and marinate the almonds for 10 minutes; then strain through a sieve and transfer to a buttered baking tray. Toast the almonds in the oven until crisp, about 15 minutes. Set aside to cool.

Remove the terrine from the mold. Using a clean knife, cut the terrine into ½-inch-thick slices, wiping the knife clean after each slice. Divide among small plates, garnish with the almonds and serve with toast or warm bread.

HEIRLOOM CARROTS CONFIT
WITH SPANAKOPITA & FARMER'S CHEESE DOLMA

Gently poached in olive oil and redolent of aromatic spices, the carrots confit is a wonderful focal point around which to build a dish. I've brought together other elements to provide variety, texture and flavor.

SERVES 8

3 cups heirloom carrots

sea salt

olive oil

2 pieces star anise

6 cardamom pods

2 tablespoons orange zest

1 cup quinoa

¼ cup toasted amaranth

¼ cup toasted sesame seeds

½ cup chopped fresh parsley

1 tablespoon minced fresh mint

¼ cup finely diced cucumbers

¼ cup diced tomatoes

2 teaspoons red wine vinegar

freshly ground black pepper

¼ cup diced salted lemons (see larder)

¼ cup olives

FOR THE SPANAKOPITA

1 medium onion, thinly sliced

2 tablespoons minced garlic

2 tablespoons sunflower oil

1 quart spinach

¼ cup heavy cream

2 teaspoons minced lemon zest

2 sheets filo dough

olive oil

¾ cup farmer's cheese (page 200)

FOR THE DOLMA

¼ cup farmer's cheese (page 200)

2 teapoons minced onion

½ teaspoon minced garlic

1 tablespoon olive oil

1 teaspoon paprika

1 teaspoon cumin

1 teaspoon coriander

½ teaspoon dill seed

8 grape leaves

In a medium saucepan over high heat, boil the carrots in salted water for 2 minutes. Drain and return to the saucepan. Add 2 cups olive oil, the spices and orange zest and cook over low heat until the carrots are tender, about 1 hour. Remove from the stove and keep warm.

In a small saucepan, boil the quinoa and amaranth in salted water until tender, about 15 minutes. Drain through a fine sieve and place in a medium bowl. Add the sesame seeds, herbs, cucumbers, tomatoes, 2 tablespoons olive oil and the vinegar. Season the tabouleh with salt and pepper and mix well.

Make the spanakopita: In a large sauté pan over high heat, cook the onion and garlic in the sunflower oil until the onion just begins to brown, about 5 minutes. Mix in the spinach and cook until wilted. Squeeze the spinach with a spatula and pour off any juices. Add the heavy cream and lemon zest and cook until thickened. Season with salt, remove from the stove and let cool.

For the dolma, in a small bowl, combine the cheese, onion, garlic, olive oil and spices. Season with salt and mix well. Lay the grape leaves out on a work surface. Place 1 tablespoon of filling onto the center of each of the grape leaves and roll up, forming packages.

Preheat the oven to 450°F.

On a clean, dry work surface, unroll and stack the filo sheets. Brush the top with some olive oil. Fold the filo in half crosswise. Brush the top again with olive oil. Beginning 2 inches from the bottom, top the filo with the spinach and farmer's cheese. Tightly roll into a long log and transfer to a baking sheet. Bake until golden, about 12 minutes. Let cool. Trim the ends and cut the spanakopita into 8 equal pieces.

Divide the carrots, dolmas, and spanakopita among eight plates. Add several spoonfuls of the tabouleh to each plate and top with the salted lemons and olives. Serve immediately.

LOBSTER QUENELLE WITH PORK BELLY

These are like eating a lobster cloud; delicate, but tasting richly of the sea. One often sees seafood and pork together in Asian cuisines. Here, lobster is partnered with tender pork belly that's been braised then chilled overnight. I use the pork broth scented with seaweed to marry the two. Marinated turnips and snow peas add complexity while keeping the dish light.

SERVES 6

½ pound fresh pork belly, cut into 1-inch pieces
sea salt
3 tablespoons sliced fresh ginger
1 medium onion, sliced
1 quart chicken stock (see larder)
1 stalk lemongrass, chopped
3 tablespoons dried kombu seaweed
¼ cup rice vinegar, plus more for seasoning
1 tablespoon dried ground wakame seaweed
½ cup heavy cream
½ pound scallops
½ pound lobster meat, picked
½ cup unsalted butter, softened
2 large eggs
3 tablespoons heavy cream, at room temperature
1 teaspoon sugar
1 teaspoons sesame oil
½ cup julienned Japanese turnips
½ cup julienned snow peas
½ cup pea vines and flowers

Preheat the oven to 200°F.

Season the pork belly with salt. In an ovenproof pan over high heat, combine the pork, 2 tablespoons of the ginger and the onion. Cook until the onions begin to brown. Add the stock, lemongrass and kombu; cover and braise in the oven for about 5 hours, until the belly is fork-tender. Remove the belly from the broth, strain the pork broth through a fine sieve and chill both, separately, overnight.

The next day, in a medium sauté pan over high heat, sear the belly until crisp on one side. Set aside in a warm place.

Remove the layer of fat from the top of the pork stock and keep for another use. Transfer the stock to a medium pot over high heat and season with salt and a dash of rice vinegar. Add the wakame and keep warm.

In a large saucepan over high heat, bring 1 quart water with the heavy cream, remaining tablespoon ginger and a pinch of salt to a boil, then reduce to a simmer. This is your poaching liquid and should be kept at a simmer throughout.

In the bowl of a food processor, combine the scallops and lobster meat and pulse until ground. Add the butter and grind for a full minute until lightened in color. Transfer to a medium bowl and mix in the eggs and cream. Season with salt, then test the seasoning by poaching a small spoonful in the poaching liquid. Adjust the seasoning as necessary.

Working in batches so as not to overcrowd the pot, scoop a tablespoon of the ground shellfish using a large soup spoon. Using an identical soup spoon, remove the mixture from the first spoon pressing to form a football shape, or quenelle, and drop into the poaching liquid. Poach the quenelles until firm, but do not let the mixture boil. When the quenelles are cooked through, gently remove them to a plate. Repeat until the ground shellfish is used up. Reduce the temperature of the poaching liquid to low and return the quenelles to the pot to stay warm.

In a medium pot over high heat, bring the remaining ¼ cup rice vinegar, sugar and sesame oil to a boil, then remove the pan from the heat. Add the turnips, season with salt and mix well. Let marinate for 10 minutes off the heat; then strain the turnips through a sieve.

Divide the pork belly among six soup bowls. Add the snow peas. Transfer the quenelles to the bowls, lightly drying them as they are removed from the poaching liquid. Garnish with the pickled turnips and the pea vines and flowers. Finally, ladle the warm pork broth over the top and serve immediately.

SPRING ON THE FARM

Hope, for me, is defined by walking into the farm's field to harvest on the first warm days of the year. Despite winter's lingering adversity, everything is possible once the season's days begin to warm. Spring combines that glowing warmth with bracing cold—sometimes on the same day. Our harvests and cooking style reflect that, too: long slow-cooked dishes and hearty broths accented with the delicate flowers and tiny leaves I crave after a long winter without.

SQUASH BLOSSOMS

Quick chilling after harvest is essential when harvesting squash blossoms. I like to harvest them early in the morning, well before the afternoon heat is on. Open each flower as you go, for occasionally you'll find a trapped bee inside.

A TRIO OF RADISHES
WITH CHICKEN & FOIE GRAS

This dish brings together three uses for radishes, yielding a spectacular result: baby radishes are sautéed, others are turned into a decadent foam, and the greens are wilted. The warm, soft poached chicken is succulent and the foie gras and truffle add elegance.

SERVES 4

2 cups White Hailstone radishes, trimmed, plus 1 cup White Hailstone radish greens
2 cups heavy cream
sea salt
2 teaspoons truffle oil
1 cup Cherry Belle radishes
2 tablespoons unsalted butter, softened
1 teaspoon sherry vinegar

1 cup spring radishes, trimmed and thinly shaved
2 tablespoons black truffles, shaved
2 tablespoons basic vinaigrette (see larder)
2 poached chicken breasts (see larder)
¼ cup salt-cured foie gras, shaved (see larder)

In a small saucepan over medium-high heat, combine the white radishes and cream and cook until very tender. Transfer to a blender and purée until very smooth, adding water if necessary. Season with salt and the truffle oil.

In a large sauté pan over high heat, sauté the Cherry Belle radishes in the butter until warmed through. Add the radish greens and cook until wilted. Remove from the heat and season with salt and the sherry vinegar.

In a small bowl, combine the spring radishes, truffles and vinaigrette. Season with salt and toss well.

Slice the chicken and divide among four small plates. Using a hand blender, froth the radish purée. Top the chicken with the radish froth. Garnish the plates with the sautéed radishes and the radish salad. Place several shards of foie gras on the plates and serve immediately.

RADISHES

Members of the mustard or brassica family, radishes fall into two basic types. Fast-growing spring radishes include the standard red supermarket varieties, as well as others in colors ranging from white to pink to purple. The texture is juicy-crisp and they have just enough heat to make them interesting. My favorites are the White Hailstone, the bright red Cherry Belle, and the gorgeous pink Sezanne. Slower-growing winter radishes, with their firmer texture and a hearty dose of spicy heat, tend to mature larger and keep well in the root cellar. For winter radishes, I'm a fan of the Münchener bier radish, misato rose and Japanese "cherry blossom" radish called Iiinona Kabu. For a simple, yet delicious snack, try tossing the radishes in salt to marinate. Then, after rinsing, serve them with soft, whipped butter. They are a joy.

SQUASH BLOSSOM FRITES WITH LEMON RICOTTA

I cook with an abundance of flowers in the kitchen. One of my favorites every year is squash blossoms. Here, I've crusted the blossoms in a polenta. The chilled, lemony ricotta adds a fresh yet rich note and the tomato fonduto adds complexity.

SERVES 4

sunflower oil
½ cup fresh ricotta (page 100)
2 teaspoons minced lemon zest
lemon juice to taste
sea salt

16 squash blossoms
½ cup rice flour
¼ cup finely ground polenta
½ cup soda water
¼ cup tomato fonduto (see larder)

Heat 2 inches oil in a pot to 375°F as measured on a deep-fry thermometer.

In a small bowl, combine the ricotta, lemon zest and lemon juice. Season with salt and mix well. Fill each squash blossom with a spoonful of the ricotta mixture.

In a second bowl, combine the rice flour, polenta and soda water. Season with salt and mix well. Dip each squash blossom into the batter, ensuring that it is fully but lightly covered with batter. Wipe off any excess and fry the blossoms, a few at a time, in the hot oil until golden, about 3 minutes. Transfer to a tray lined with paper towels to drain. Continue until all of the blossoms are used up.

Divide the squash blossoms among four plates. Garnish each with the tomato fonduto. Season with more lemon juice and serve immediately.

MADE-TO-ORDER MOZZARELLA WITH BASIL

There are dishes that get better with time, like chicken soup. Others are best as soon as they are finished—none more so than mozzarella. While chilled fresh mozzarella is wonderful, it pales compared to mozzarella right out of the pot. The technique is simple, but the results are spectacular. And, really, the main difference is nothing more than time. Order the mozzarella curd online or from your local cheesemonger.

SERVES 4

1 cup fresh basil leaves
½ cup spinach leaves
2 ice cubes
2 tablespoons sunflower oil
sea salt

1 teaspoon lemon juice
1 tablespoon salt
2 cups mozzarella curd, crumbled
3 tablespoons olive oil

In a blender, combine the basil, spinach, ice and oil. Purée at high speed until very smooth. Strain through a fine-mesh strainer into a small bowl and season with salt and the lemon juice.

In a small saucepan, heat 3 cups of water to 140 to 160°F, which is too hot to touch with bare hands but cooler than a simmer. Season with enough salt that the water tastes of the sea. Add the mozzarella curd and cook, stirring gently, until the curds have melted. Working quickly, remove the curds to a work surface, cut into 4 equal pieces and form into balls. The more the curd is worked, the firmer and drier it becomes. I prefer the curd worked as little as possible, so the cheese has a cloud-like texture.

Place the mozzarella in four warmed bowls. Top with the olive oil and drizzle with the basil purée. Serve immediately.

FENNEL FLAN WITH TOMATO CONSOMMÉ & TOMATO TART TATIN

I've taken classics from the dessert world and moved them to the savory end of the table with this dish. First is a remake of flan, the classic Spanish dessert custard. Alongside goes a savory tart tatin, with heirloom tomatoes and Parmesan standing in for the apple and caramel. A fresh tomato "consommé," which needs to drain overnight, adds brightness and acidity and, finally, some shaved fennel, a playful texture.

SERVES 4

1 pound heirloom tomatoes, trimmed
¼ cup diced fennel stalks
sea salt
2 bulbs fennel, sliced, plus ½ cup shaved fennel
2 tablespoons sunflower oil
2 cups heavy cream
1 large egg
3 egg yolks
1 teaspoon fresh lemon juice
4 Black Prince tomatoes, cut into 1-inch-thick slices
2 tablespoons grated Parmesan cheese
2 teaspoons capers, drained
4 ounces frozen thawed puff pastry dough, rolled thinly and cut into quarters
12 cherry tomatoes
1 tablespoon basic vinaigrette (see larder)

In a blender, purée the heirloom tomatoes and fennel stalks at high speed until very smooth. Transfer to a colander lined with cheesecloth set over a medium bowl and place in the refrigerator overnight to drain. Once drained, season with salt. (Hint: The remaining solids make a good start for homemade tomato sauce.)

Preheat the oven to 200°F.

In a small saucepan over high heat, cook the sliced fennel bulbs in 1 tablespoon of the sunflower oil until the fennel just begins to color, about 3 minutes. Reduce the heat to low and add the heavy cream. Simmer for 20 minutes, then remove the saucepan from the heat and let cool.

Strain the cream into a medium bowl, discarding the solids. Add the egg and eggs yolks and stir well. Season with salt and the lemon juice. Divide the mixture among four flan dishes or similar bowls. Place in a roasting pan and add water to the pan to make a bain marie. Lightly cover the roasting pan with aluminum foil and bake until the flans have set, about 1 hour.

Increase the oven temperature to 500°F.

In a medium bowl, combine the Black Prince tomatoes and remaining 1 tablespoon sunflower oil and season with salt. Toss well, then spread the tomatoes on a baking sheet in a single layer. Bake until they just begin to brown, about 8 minutes. Remove from the oven and let cool. Top the tomatoes with the Parmesan, capers and pastry dough. Return to the oven and bake until the crusts are golden, about 8 minutes more. Let cool.

In a small bowl, combine the shaved fennel, cherry tomatoes and vinaigrette. Season with salt and toss well.

Unmold the flans into four soup bowls. Place a tomato tart alongside. Garnish with the shaved fennel and tomato salad. Finally, pour the tomato consommé into the bowls and serve immediately.

CILANTRO

Each morning, I quietly walk the farm's vegetable rows while I have my morning coffee. I use the time to taste little bits here and there from the vegetables as I begin to plan the day. It is an important time for adjusting what we are serving in the restaurant. The flavors I taste on these morning walks are the seeds of new dishes for the coming days—and that is how this fluke crudo with cilantro flowers came about. While walking along the rows of cilantro that had begun to bolt, I took a chance nip of a cilantro flower. It exploded with the flavor of fresh, vivid cilantro but looked so delicate. For most of the day, I played with the flavor in my head. By late afternoon, I was ready to start testing this dish.

FLUKE CRUDO WITH CILANTRO FLOWERS & AVOCADO

The dish is really quite simple. Cut thin enough to see through, the raw fluke has a buttery texture. Delicate cilantro flowers explode with herbal cilantro notes. Nasturtium leaves and flowers add a peppery spice and the avocado and lime bring the elements together.

SERVES 4

1 cup nasturtium leaves and flowers
1 tablespoon olive oil
lime juice to taste
sea salt

6 ounces sashimi grade fluke, thinly sliced
1 avocado, sliced
3 tablespoons cilantro flowers (see note, opposite)

In a small bowl, combine the nasturtium leaves and olive oil. Season with lime juice and salt and toss well.

Divide among four chilled plates. Top with the slices of fish and avocado and season with more lime juice and salt. Garnish with the cilantro flowers and serve immediately.

DUCK CONFIT WITH GRILLED PEACHES & GINGER GASTRIQUE

A balance of light, summery flavors and rich, decadent ones, this dish pairs an aromatic duck confit with ripe sweet peaches bursting with juice that pick up a smoky hint after a little time spent on the grill. Cool summer lettuces keep the dish light and the spicy-sweet ginger gastrique adds a bright acidity.

SERVES 4

1 cup white vinegar
½ cup sugar
2 tablespoons thinly sliced fresh ginger
4 peaches, halved and pitted

4 duck confit legs (see larder)
4 cups summer lettuces
1 tablespoon basic vinaigrette (see larder)

In a small pot over high heat, combine the vinegar, sugar and ginger. Cook until reduced by half and thickened. Set aside (see note).

Over a charcoal or wood fire, grill the peach halves and duck legs until lightly charred and warmed through, about 4 minutes.

In a medium bowl, toss the lettuces with the vinaigrette. Divide among four plates and top each with the peaches and duck. Drizzle with the ginger gastrique and serve immediately.

CANDIED GINGER

Often the byproducts of one prized dish are like gold in their own right, which is the case with the leftover ginger from making this ginger gastrique. After prolonged cooking, the ginger is candied with a wonderful sweet-sour-spicy balance. I remove it from the gastrique to drain and cool a bit, then I dredge the pieces through a bowl of sugar before letting them dry for an hour or two. Delicious for snacking, I also use it atop desserts like the carrot cake on page 227.

STUFFED SUMMER SQUASH
WITH RATATOUILLE & TALEGGIO

Ratatouille is breathtaking when you think of the hours and hours of sunshine concentrated into a single spoonful. It really is a marvel. I like to highlight ratatouille in this spectacular dish as a celebration of the end of summer.

SERVES 6 TO 8

2 cups diced summer squash

2 cups peeled and diced eggplant

2 cups diced red peppers

3 cups diced tomatoes

2 medium onions, diced

¼ cup minced garlic

1 large fennel bulb, diced

¼ cup olive oil

2 bay leaves

1 sprig fresh rosemary

6 sprigs fresh thyme

¼ cup chopped fresh basil, plus ¼ cup fresh basil leaves

12 small round summer squashes, like Eight Ball or Ronde de Nice

2 tablespoons sunflower oil

sea salt

¼ cup Taleggio cheese, cut into thin slices

¼ cup basil coulis (see larder)

Preheat the oven to 400°F.

Working in batches, in a large sauté pan over high heat, sauté the diced squash, eggplant, peppers, tomatoes, onions, garlic and fennel in the olive oil until lightly browned. Transfer to a baking dish, add the bay leaves and rosemary and bake until a crust forms on the top, about 1 hour. Stir the vegetables, mixing in the crust, and bake 30 minutes more. Remove from the oven and stir in the thyme and chopped basil. Set aside.

Cut the tops off of the squashes. Using a spoon or melon baller, hollow out the centers of each squash. Place the hollowed squashes and tops in a medium bowl, dress with the sunflower oil and toss well to coat. Season with salt.

Spread out the squash on a baking sheet in a single layer. Bake in the oven until just tender, about 6 minutes.

Fill the squash cups with the ratatouille. Top with the Taleggio and return to the oven until the cheese has melted, about 5 minutes more.

Divide the squash among warmed plates. Garnish with the basil leaves and basil coulis. Serve immediately.

- -

SUMMER SQUASH

Despite the lack of rhyming, "you say summer squash, I say zucchini" should have been included in the song "Let's Call the Whole Thing Off" because they really are the same thing. We grow about twelve varieties at the farm, in every color and shape: the traditional long "zucchinis," crooknecks, scalloped pattypan and round squash (Eight Ball, One Ball and Ronde di Nice), which I love for this recipe as they make perfect vessels for baking when hollowed out. Most summer squashes are part of the Cucurbita pepo group, like acorn squash, and develop a hard shell and tough seeds if left to mature on the vine too long. Because their flavor and texture are better when small, before the seeds have developed, we harvest them almost every day. For best flavor, try the light green varieties like Costata Romanesca, Lounge Fiorentino and Cocozelle—very old traditional European types. American supermarket owners don't like them as they bruise easily, so the dark green color was bred in to mask the bruising, and the flavor was lost in the bargain.

SCALLOPS À LA PLANCHA
WITH SWEET CORN SUCCOTASH

Plump diver scallops benefit greatly from cooking on a hot plancha or cast-iron skillet. Their natural sugars caramelize quickly, heightening flavor. After the quick sear, the residual heat is enough to cook the scallops to perfect doneness after a few moments rest. Here, I've paired the scallops with a quickly cooked succotash of grilled sweet corn and fresh heirloom broad beans. The shaved bits of speck further enhance the smokiness of the dish.

SERVES 4

¼ cup minced onion

¼ cup minced leek

1 tablespoon minced garlic

¼ cup plus 1 tablespoon
   unsalted butter, softened

1 cup white wine

2 tablespoons heavy cream

1 cup fresh broad beans,
   shelled

1 cup grilled corn kernels

½ cup shaved speck

1 tablespoon minced rosemary

sea salt

8 large scallops, rinsed

1 tablespoon sunflower oil

In a small saucepan over medium heat, cook the onion, leek and garlic in 1 tablespoon of the butter until the garlic just begins to turn golden, about 3 minutes. Pour in the wine and cook until reduced by three-quarters, about 10 minutes. Reduce the heat to low and add the heavy cream, beans, corn, speck, rosemary and the remaining ¼ cup butter. Cook, stirring constantly, until the butter has just melted but has not separated, about 4 minutes. Season with salt and remove the pan from the heat but keep warm.

Season the scallops with salt. In a heavy cast-iron skillet over high heat, cook the scallops in the oil until golden, about 3 minutes per side. Transfer the scallops to the butter mixture and let rest for 3 minutes. For smaller scallops, cook only on one side.

Divide the scallops and buttery corn and beans among four plates. Serve immediately.

COOKING TIP

I learned the joy of grilled sweet corn from my grandfather. At our big family summer cookouts, he would casually toss ears of sweet corn, minutes after harvest, into the great wood fire he used for grilling meats. The first time I saw him do this I thought he was crazy.
"Hey, Papa! You missed the grill and the ears of corn dropped right into the fire!" He solemnly placed them in a paper bag and said, "Peel these burned ones open and see if there is anything we can salvage." As I peeled away the charred outer layers, I got to the inside, which yielded bright white kernels with a touch of a golden hue from the roasting and a faint smoky-sweet aroma. They were perfection. Even today, I'm still surprised to see the clean, pearly corn beneath the charred husks. Peeling back that last blackened layer is like redemption.

PORK BELLY WITH YELLOW SPLIT PEAS & YOGURT SAUCE

Pork belly is uncured bacon that is usually braised or poached and then chilled overnight. As it is quite rich, a little goes a long way. I like to pair it with ingredients that lighten it up with bright flavors and crunchy textures. The spiced yellow peas add background aromas and the yogurt cuts through the richness of the pork belly. Roasted cabbage adds a pleasant umami and smoky flavor.

SERVES 4

1 pound fresh pork belly, cut into 1-inch pieces

sea salt

2 tablespoons sliced fresh ginger

1 medium onion, sliced, plus 1 medium onion, diced

1 carrot, trimmed and sliced

1 rib celery, sliced

1 quart pork or chicken stock (see larder)

1 cup sliced napa cabbage

1 tablespoon minced garlic

1 tablespoon sunflower oil

1 cup yellow split peas

1 teaspoon ground cumin

1 teaspoon ground coriander

¼ teaspoon ground cardamom

lemon juice to taste

1 cup plain yogurt

½ cup diced cucumber

1 tablespoon chopped fresh dill

1 tablespoon chopped fresh cilantro, plus 2 tablespoons leaves for garnish

1 tablespoon chopped fresh mint

1 tablespoon garlic oil (see larder)

freshly ground black pepper

1 tablespoon diced scallion

Preheat the oven to 200°F.

Season the pork belly with salt. In an ovenproof braising pan over high heat, combine the belly pieces, 1 tablespoon of the ginger, the sliced onion, carrot and celery. Cook until the onions begin to brown. Add the stock and cabbage; cover and put the braising pan in the oven. Braise until the belly is fork tender, about 5 hours. Remove the belly from the broth, strain the pork broth through a fine sieve and chill both, separately, in the refrigerator overnight.

The next day, in a medium sauté pan over high heat, sear the belly until crisp on one side. Keep the seared belly pieces in a warm place.

In a medium saucepan over high heat, combine the diced onion, garlic, the remaining 1 tablespoon ginger and oil. Cook until the onions just begin to color, about 7 minutes. Mix in the split peas and spices and cook until the spices are aromatic, about 2 minutes more. Pour in enough reserved pork stock to cover and cook, stirring often, until the lentils are very tender, about 30 minutes. Season with salt and lemon juice.

In a medium bowl, combine the yogurt, cucumber, herbs and garlic oil. Season with salt and pepper and mix well.

Divide the yellow peas among four small plates. Top with the pork belly. Garnish with the yogurt sauce, cilantro and scallions and serve immediately.

VARIATIONS OF BEETS
WITH TREVISO & GORGONZOLA

At the farm, we grow a broad variety of heirloom beets. Some are the old stalwarts like Detroit Red, some are colorful and exotic like the hot pink Three Root Grex or Giante Blanche. Each year, I put together a dish that highlights the different types together.

SERVES 6

SALT-ROASTED BEETS

2 large red beets such as
    Detroit or Early Tall Top
2 large Chiogga beets
2 large Three Root Grex beets
7 cups salt
¼ cup basic vinaigrette
    (see larder)

BEET NAPOLEONS

2 bay leaves
1 piece star anise
2 cardamom pods
1 tablespoon black
    peppercorns
1 cup baby beets, peeled
    and trimmed
2 tablespoons red wine
    vinegar
1 tablespoon honey
½ cup Gorgonzola cheese,
    softened
¼ cup heavy cream

First, prepare the salt-roasted beets: Preheat the oven to 400°F. Place the beets in a baking dish. Top with the salt, burying the beets underneath. Bake until very tender, about 1 hour. Remove the beets from the salt and let cool. Peel the beets and rinse the excess salt off with water. Thinly slice using a mandolin, placing each beet color in a different bowl. Dress all in the vinaigrette.

Next prepare the beet napoleons: On a 7-inch piece of cheesecloth, combine the bay leaves and spices to form a bundle. Place in a medium saucepan with 1 cup water and the beets, vinegar and honey. Cook over high heat until tender, about 40 minutes. Strain the beets through a colander and discard the spice bundle. Slice the beets into ¼-inch-thick slices.

In the bowl of a food processor, purée the cheese and heavy cream until smooth and lightened. Place a little scoop of the cheese on top of the beet slices. Stack the beet slices to form 6 napoleons. Refrigerate for 40 minutes, until set.

For the pickled beets, in a medium saucepan over high heat, combine the beets with 2 cups water, the lemon juice and a pinch of salt and boil until tender, about 35 minutes. Strain and let cool. Peel the beets, then place in a small bowl with the vinegar and tarragon. Season with salt and marinate for 30 minutes.

Transfer one of the beets to the bowl of a food processor with the crème fraîche and goat cheese. Purée until very smooth. Season with salt and chill in the refrigerator until firm, about 40 minutes.

Cut the remaining beets into 1-inch-thick slices. Using a vegetable peeler or paring knife, cut the beet slices into long spiral strips at least 4 inches long. Lay the strips out on a clean work surface. Spread a thin layer of the goat cheese mixture on a strip and roll it up, jelly-roll style. Trim the ends with a clean, sharp knife. Drizzle the tops with the walnut oil and season with the pepper.

In a medium sauté pan over high heat, sauté the shallots in the butter until they begin to brown, about 4 minutes. Add 1 cup of the treviso, the wine and heavy cream. Reduce the heat to low and cook until thickened, about 7 minutes. Season with salt and nutmeg and mix well. Cool to room temperature.

On a clean work surface, lay out 6 slices of the salt-roasted chioggia beets. Top each with a spoonful of the cooled treviso. Top with a second beet slice to form raviolis.

PICKLED WHITE BEETS AND WHITE BEET MOUSSE

2 large white beets, such as
   Giante Blanche, peeled
2 tablespoons lemon juice
sea salt
2 tablespoons champagne
   vinegar
1 sprig tarragon
¼ cup crème fraîche
2 tablespoons goat cheese
1 tablespoon walnut oil
1 teaspoon freshly ground
   black pepper

2 shallots, sliced
1 tablespoon unsalted butter
1½ cups radicchio di Treviso
   leaves
2 tablespoons white wine
2 tablespoons heavy cream
sea salt
freshly grated nutmeg to taste
2 tablespoons roasted garlic
   oil (see larder)
1 tablespoon grated orange
   zest
¼ cup various colors of beets,
   very finely diced
1 tablespoons walnut oil
1 teaspoon sherry vinegar
½ cup frisée leaves, washed
   and dried
½ cup Bull's Blood beet leaves,
   washed and dried
1 tablespoons basic vinaigrette
   (see larder)

Cut the salt-roasted Detroit and Grex beets into 1½-inch-thick slices. Using a paring knife or peeler, cut the beets into long spiraling strips. Dress the beets with the garlic oil and orange zest and roll each strip into a spiral.

In a small bowl, combine the diced beets, walnut oil and vinegar. Season with salt and mix well.

In a medium bowl, combine the frisée, beet leaves and vinaigrette. Season with salt and toss well.

Divide and arrange the various beet components among six large salad plates. Garnish with the dressed leaves and serve immediately.

LAMB CARPACCIO WITH HARISSA & CRISP CAPERS

While the texture of carpaccio is great, I've often felt that it lacks flavor. To overcome this, I've heavily seasoned the lamb with freshly cracked pepper and given it a very brief sear on a very hot grill. These added steps boost the lamb's flavor tremendously. The spicy harissa, a Moroccan condiment, adds an exotic note, while the crisp capers add a crunchy, salty texture.

SERVES 4

3 tablespoons sunflower oil

2 tablespoons capers, drained and patted dry

8 ounces lamb loin

sea salt and freshly ground black pepper

1 cup diced carrot

¼ cup sliced onion

2 tablespoons minced garlic

1 teaspoon ground caraway

2 teaspoons dried chiles

1 teaspoon ground cumin

1 teaspoon ground coriander

¼ cup olive oil

lemon juice to taste

2 tablespoons chopped fresh cilantro

In a medium sauté pan over high heat, heat the oil to 375°F, as measured on a deep-fry thermometer. Crisp the capers in the oil, for about 1 minute. Transfer to paper towels to drain.

Season the lamb liberally with salt and pepper. Return the sauté pan to the stove over high heat and briefly sear the lamb for about 30 seconds per side; the lamb should still be raw on the inside. Transfer to a small tray lined with plastic wrap and place in the freezer to chill until the lamb is partially frozen. It should have a slushy feel. Remove the lamb from the freezer and slice it crosswise as thinly as possible; the slices should be a little thicker than sheets of paper.

In a medium saucepan over high heat, combine the carrot, onion and garlic and spices. Cover with water and cook until the water has fully reduced and the carrots are very tender. Transfer to a blender and purée until very smooth. With the motor running, drizzle in 2 tablespoons of the olive oil. Season with the lemon juice and salt. Transfer the carrot harissa to a squeeze bottle or small tightly sealed plastic container and chill in the refrigerator.

Lay out the sliced lamb on four chilled plates and top with dots of the harissa sauce. Garnish with the capers, remaining olive oil and cilantro leaves. Serve immediately.

POULTRY

IF THE FIRST YEAR'S GARDEN WAS A SLIPPERY SLOPE TOWARDS FARMING, THEN IT WAS RAISING OUR FIRST ROOSTER, NAMED BABAGANOUJ, THAT MADE IT A STEEP SLOPE, INDEED. GORGEOUS PLUMAGE AND AN EASY DEMEANOR ENDEARED BABAGANOUJ TO US AS HE AND HIS GIRLS BROUGHT LIFE TO THE FARMHOUSE'S YARD. FROM HIM, WE LEARNED THAT POULTRY NEEDS TO BE RAISED OUTDOORS IN FRESH PASTURES. THE ANIMALS ARE HEALTHIER, HAPPIER, AND TASTE BETTER.

DUCK WITH JURANÇON, APRICOTS & CHARD

Jurançon, the unsung dessert wine of the French Basque region, is a stunning partner for roasted duck. I use it to poach apricots and then for a quick pan sauce. Each time I make this dish, I am reminded of the rolling hills of the region, and of course, the spectacular food!

SERVES 4

2 cups Jurançon wine

2 tablespoons sugar

4 apricots

4 duck breasts, trimmed and scored

sea salt

4 tablespoons minced shallots

2 tablespoons crushed hazelnuts

3 tablespoons unsalted butter, softened, plus more for sautéeing

2 teaspoons minced garlic

3 cups chopped chard leaves

In a small saucepan over high heat, bring the wine and sugar to a boil. Reduce the heat to a simmer, add the apricots and cook for 1 minute. Using a hand strainer, transfer the apricots to a platter to cool and reserve the wine. Once the apricots are cool enough to handle, remove the skins, cut the apricots in half and remove the pits.

Season the duck with salt on both sides. In a stainless steel sauté pan over medium-low heat, gently cook the duck, skin side down, pouring off the rendered fat occasionally, until the fat is fully rendered and the skin becomes crisp, about 20 minutes. Turn the breasts over, increase the heat to high and cook until the breasts firm up a bit, about 3 minutes more. The duck will be medium rare at this point; adjust the cooking time to suit your taste. Remove the breasts from the pan to a warm place to rest for 5 minutes.

Return the pan to the heat and add half of the shallots. Cook until they just begin to brown, about 2 minutes. Pour in the reserved wine and reduce by three-quarters. Add the hazelnuts and 3 tablespoons butter, remove the pan from the heat and stir well. Add the poached apricots and season with salt.

In a large sauté pan over high heat, cook the remaining half of the shallots in a dab of butter until just beginning to brown, about 2 minutes. Add the garlic and a bit more butter and cook for 1 minute more. Add the chard and 2 tablespoons water and cook until fully wilted, about 3 minutes. Season with salt.

Slice the duck very thinly crosswise and divide among four plates. Top each with the sauce and apricots. Garnish with the chard and serve immediately.

CHICKEN WITH GARLIC SCAPE PURÉE

Part of the garlic-growing process is to remove the scapes, or necks, that eventually produce seeds. This focuses the plant's energy on sizing up the bulb. The scapes are delicious with a strong garlic flavor balanced by a green vegetal note. After cooking to soften the scapes' texture, the strong garlic flavor mellows a bit but the vegetal note carries on pleasantly. Young, green garlic scapes star in this dish as a base for the purée. The Gorgonzola adds a burst of acidity and complexity for balance while the lemon and arugula help clean the palate. The combination is a winner.

SERVES 4

4 heads young green garlic, thinly sliced (see page 95)

8 tablespoons (1 stick) unsalted butter

1 cup white wine

1 clove

1 teaspoon peppercorns

sea salt

2 cups chopped garlic scapes

1 medium potato, peeled and diced

½ cup heavy cream

4 skin-on chicken breasts

2 tablespoons minced young garlic tops

2 tablespoons minced fresh parsley

1 tablespoons minced fresh sage

lemon juice to taste

freshly ground black pepper

2 cups baby arugula

2 teaspoons basic vinaigrette (see larder)

2 tablespoons minced lemon zest

¼ cup crumbled Gorgonzola cheese

In a small saucepan over high heat, cook the garlic in 2 tablespoons of the butter until translucent, about 1 minute. Add the wine and spices and cook until fully reduced, about 10 minutes. Season with salt and set the garlic confit aside.

In a medium saucepan over high heat, cook the garlic scapes and potato in 2 tablespoons butter until the scapes just begin to brown, about 4 minutes. Add enough water to cover and boil until reduced by three-quarters. While still hot, transfer to a food processor and purèe until very smooth, about 5 minutes. Add the cream, pulsing to combine. Season with salt and set aside in a warm place.

In a large sauté pan over high heat, sauté the chicken in the remaining 4 tablespoons butter until browned, about 6 minutes. Turn the chicken breasts over, reduce the heat to medium-low and cook until firm to the touch. To be certain the chicken is done, slice open a breast—the breast should have just lost its glassy raw appearance but still be pink. Add the herbs to the pan and season with lemon juice, salt and pepper, and then remove the pan from the heat to rest. The chicken will continue to cook as the pan cools without becoming dry.

In a medium bowl, combine the arugula and vinaigrette. Season with salt and toss well.

Divide the garlic purée among four warmed plates. Top with a chicken breast, some garlic confit, the lemon zest, cheese and dressed arugula. Serve immediately.

CHICKEN POACHED IN SAFFRON OIL
WITH SPRING PEA CONSOMMÉ

This unique cooking technique yields stunning results. I love the deep perfume and soft, juicy texture poaching in saffron imparts to chicken. I've paired it with a light consommé of spring peas and a scattering of slow-cooked shallots. The wakame adds a playful crunch and umami flavor.

SERVES 4

6 shallots, peeled and trimmed

3 cups plus 1 tablespoon sunflower oil

2 bay leaves

3 cups chicken stock (see larder)

2 tablespoons verjus

sea salt and freshly ground black pepper

2 cups spring peas

2 tablespoons roasted garlic (see larder)

6 ice cubes

1 tablespoon saffron

1 tablespoon brandy

4 boneless, skinless chicken breasts

2 tablespoons dried ground wakame seaweed

In a small pot over medium heat, cook the shallots in 1 tablespoon of the oil until golden, about 2 minutes. Add the bay leaves, 2 cups of the stock and verjus and cook until fully reduced, about 20 minutes. Season with salt and pepper. Remove from the heat and set aside.

In a small pot over high heat, bring the remaining 1 cup stock plus ½ cup water to a boil. Remove from the heat and add the peas. Let rest for 1 minute then transfer the peas and liquid to a blender. Add the garlic and ice. Blend until very smooth, about 5 minutes. Season with salt, then transfer the pea purée to a colander lined with cheesecloth. Set aside to drain fully, about 1 hour. Discard the solids and set aside.

Meanwhile, in a small bowl, combine the saffron and brandy. Let the saffron bloom for about 10 minutes. Transfer to a medium pot, pour in the remaining 3 cups oil and heat over medium until the oil reaches a temperature of 160°F, as measured by a deep-fry thermometer. Season the chicken with salt and carefully slip the breasts into the oil. Cook until the internal temperature of the chicken reaches 160°F, about 35 minutes. Transfer to a warm platter.

Gently warm the pea consommé in a small pot until just warm. Divide among four warmed bowls. Top with the poached chicken, garnish with the shallots and wakame and serve immediately.

GRILLED CHICKEN
WITH COUNTRY HAM & BEANS

This is a great summery dish, combining smoky aromas and the bright, fresh notes of grilled summer beans. Pistachio tarator adds complexity to the dish without making it heavy.

SERVES 4

4 boneless chicken breasts	sea salt
2 tablespoons fresh parsley leaves	3 cups assorted summer beans, picked
1 tablespoon plus 2 teaspoons fresh thyme leaves	1 tablespoon sunflower oil
	½ cup thinly shaved and julienned country ham
2 tablespoons olive oil	1 teaspoon basic vinaigrette (see larder)
1 tablespoon minced garlic	¼ cup pistachio tarator (see larder)

In a medium bowl, combine the chicken, parsley, 1 tablespoon of the thyme, the oil and garlic and season with salt. Mix well and marinate for 1 hour in the refrigerator.

Remove the chicken from the refrigerator. On a grill, start a wood or charcoal fire. When the fire has died down to coals, it is ready for cooking. Grill the chicken for 10 minutes, turning often, until the juices run clear. Alternatively, you can cook the chicken in a broiler. Set aside on a cutting board.

In a medium bowl, combine the beans and oil. Season with salt and toss well. Place in a wire grilling basket or in foil and grill or broil the beans.

In a small bowl, toss together the ham, remaining 2 teaspoons thyme and vinaigrette. Add the beans and mix well.

Divide the chicken between four plates. Garnish with the pistachio tarator and bean mixture. Serve immediately.

TURKEY ROASTED
IN A BLANKET OF HERBS

Many vegetables, like fava beans, don't fall into a tidy three-month season; instead it's a small window of a few glorious weeks. Here, I combine them with chamomile and young garlic that share the same microseason.

SERVES 4

1 cup fresh parsley leaves	1 medium onion, diced
2 tablespoons fresh sage	¼ cup minced garlic
1 tablespoon fresh lovage leaves	1 tablespoon sunflower oil
¼ cup spring onions	1 quart turkey or chicken stock (see larder)
¼ cup young garlic	1 bay leaf
2 tablespoons unsalted butter, softened	1 cup fresh chamomile blossoms, or 2 bags of chamomile tea
1 whole heritage turkey breast, about 5 pounds	lemon juice to taste
sea salt	2 cups peeled fresh fava beans
4 ounces caul fat, rinsed	

Preheat the oven to 400°F.

In a small bowl, mix together the herbs, spring onions, young garlic and 1 tablespoon of the butter.

Season the turkey with salt. Rub the herb butter under the turkey's skin. Wrap the breast with the caul fat and place in a baking dish. Bake for 45 minutes, or until the juices run clear. Set aside on a cutting board.

In a medium saucepan over high heat, sauté the onion and garlic in the oil until translucent, about 2 minutes. Pour in the stock, add the bay leaf and cook for 20 minutes. Add the chamomile, reduce the heat to low and cook for 10 minutes. Pour through a sieve into a bowl and season with lemon juice and salt.

In a medium sauté pan over high heat, sauté the fava beans in the remaining 1 tablespoon butter until tender, about 3 minutes. Season with salt.

Slice the turkey into thin slices. Divide among four warmed plates. Garnish with the fava beans and a drizzle of the chamomile broth. Serve immediately.

SUMMER ON THE FARM

"Make hay while the sun shines," my grandfather used to say. How aptly it describes our farm each summer. The weeks change from glowing warm to intensely hot. While the sweet tomatoes and crisp summer beans destined for the July or August dinner table grow to perfection, the pressure is on to grow vegetables that sustain our restaurants through the cold months as well. Like with the pumpkins or parsnips we'll use in November, much of the fields are devoted to the future. Of course, we make hay, too, as the animals will need something to eat in the winter. After spending a morning in the field heat, my thoughts are on dinners that cool and refresh. Simple meats off the grill paired with crisp, chilled vegetables suit me during the summer.

YOUNG (OR GREEN) GARLIC

In the kitchen, garlic has a more interesting story than just the papery cloves we normally see. Traditionally, garlic is planted in the fall and grows slowly through the winter. In the spring, the plant sends up leaves reminiscent of baby leeks. To hold up its flower, the plant produces a firm stalk, or scape. The whole plant can be eaten and tastes pleasantly like garlic. I love to use scapes for purées and soups. I also mince and toss the leaves into salads in lieu of chives. The flowers are perfect on top of crispy potato latkes or with lox on a bagel. My favorite beyond-the-clove use for garlic, though, is for young garlic bulbs—simply a garlic plant harvested before the bulb is fully mature. As the papery cover on the cloves has not fully formed, there is no need to peel, making prep time a snap. Young garlic retains an herbal note that I find endearing. I often make a risotto flavored with the chopped tops that highlights their refreshing, spicy, vegetal note. Or, I'll pickle fingernail-sized heads to use as a foil for rich meats.

GRILLED DUCK & FIGS
WITH BARBERA SAUCE & LAVENDER HONEY

A touch of sweetness is often just the thing for roasted duck. Here, I've scented honey with the enigmatic aroma of lavender. The combination is stunning, lifting the peppery roasted duck to a new level. The vivid, deeply concentrated Barbera wine reduction and the earthy sweetness of the grilled figs add a level of seriousness to this elegant dish.

SERVES 4

¼ cup clover honey
1 tablespoon fresh lavender flowers
12 fresh figs, trimmed
1 tablespoon sunflower oil
4 duck breasts, trimmed and scored
sea salt

BARBERA SAUCE
2 cups duck stock or chicken stock (see larder)
2 cups Barbera wine
1 large onion, diced
1 carrot, sliced
2 ribs celery, diced
2 bay leaves
1 tablespoon peppercorns
1 tablespoon sunflower oil
sea salt
4 sprigs fresh thyme

In a small bowl, combine the honey and lavender and marinate for 2 hours.

Meanwhile, make the Barbera sauce: In a medium pot over high heat, bring the stock and wine to a boil. Reduce by half, about 1 hour, skimming the top to remove any scum that forms.

On a grill, start a wood or charcoal fire. When the fire has died down to coals it is ready for cooking.

In a medium sauté pan over high heat, combine the onion, carrots, celery, bay leaves, peppercorns and oil. Cook until the onion browns, about 10 minutes. Add the vegetables to the stock and reduce the temperature to a simmer. Cook for 30 minutes; then strain the stock through a fine sieve, discarding the solids. Season with salt, add the thyme and keep warm

In a small bowl, toss together the figs and oil. Grill the figs over the charcoal or wood fire until lightly charred and warmed through; set aside.

Season the duck with salt on both sides. In a stainless-steel sauté pan over medium-low heat, gently cook the duck, skin side down, pouring the fat off occasionally, until the fat is fully rendered and the skin has become crisp, about 20 minutes. Transfer the breasts to the charcoal or wood fire and cook, skin side up, until the breasts begin to firm up and are pink inside, 3 to 4 minutes more. Transfer to a platter and lightly coat the breasts with the lavender honey. Let rest in a warm place for 5 minutes.

Slice the duck breasts crosswise into very thin slices. Divide the duck and the figs among four plates. Top the duck with the Barbera sauce and serve immediately.

TRUFFLED DUCK BREAST
WITH PLUMS, HARICOT VERTS & FOIE GRAS

Our forager, Colin, brings us a small amount of French prune plums each fall. I love to dry them slowly in the oven where they develop a buttery texture and the perfect balance between sweet and tart. Paired with duck, I think they are perfection.

SERVES 4

¼ cup wild flower honey

1 tablespoon minced black truffle

1 tablespoon black truffle oil

1½ cups haricot verts, trimmed

sea salt

4 duck breasts, trimmed and scored

2 medium shallots, minced

2 tablespoons unsalted butter, softened

2 teaspoons champagne vinegar

4 ounces cured foie gras, thinly shaved (see larder)

PINOT NOIR SAUCE

2 cups duck stock or chicken stock (see larder)

2 cups Pinot Noir wine

4 Friar plums, halved

2 tablespoons sunflower oil

1 large onion, diced

1 carrot, sliced

2 ribs celery, diced

2 bay leaves

1 tablespoon peppercorns

sea salt

3 sprigs fresh thyme

In a small bowl, combine the honey, black truffle and oil. Mix well and marinate for 2 hours.

Meanwhile, get the Pinot Noir sauce going: In a medium pot over high heat, bring the stock and wine to a boil. Cook to reduce by half, about 1 hour, skimming the stock to remove any scum that forms.

Preheat the oven to 200°F. Toss the plums in 1 tablespoon of the oil and place on a baking sheet. Bake until somewhat dried, about 30 minutes. Let cool.

In a medium sauté pan over high heat, combine the onion, carrot, celery, bay leaves, peppercorns and remaining tablespoon oil. Cook until the onion begins to brown, about 4 minutes. Add the vegetables to the stock and reduce the heat to a simmer. Cook for 30 minutes, then strain through a fine sieve, discarding the solids. Return the sauce to the pot, season with salt, add the thyme and plums and keep warm.

Blanch the haricots verts in a pot of boiling salted water for 30 seconds, then transfer to a bowl of ice water. Strain and dry.

Season the duck with salt on both sides. In a stainless-steel sauté pan over medium-low heat, gently cook the duck, skin side down, pouring off the rendered fat occasionally, until the fat is fully rendered and the skin becomes crisp, about 20 minutes. Turn the breasts over and cook until the breasts firm up and are pink inside, about 3 minutes more. Remove the breasts from the pan to a warm place to rest for 5 minutes. Coat with the truffled honey.

Return the sauté pan to high heat. Add the shallots, butter and haricots verts and cook until the shallots begin to color and the haricots verts are warmed through, about 3 minutes. Season with salt and add the vinegar.

Thinly slice the duck breasts crosswise and divide among four plates. Garnish with the haricots verts, Pinot Noir sauce and plums. Top each plate with the foie gras shavings and serve immediately.

BUTTERMILK POACHED TURKEY
WITH SPICED EGGPLANT & ONION BEIGNETS

Turkey in America comes on a platter of great expectations wrapped in a long tradition. As a result, in the restaurant I feature turkey in out-of-the-box dishes using unique flavors and uncommon cooking techniques. Already rich in flavor, the turkey gets a boost from the buttermilk poaching liquid used in this dish. Spiced eggplant adds a strong contrast while the onion "beignets" add a pleasing textural foil.

SERVES 4

3 cups eggplant, cubed

2 tablespoons sunflower oil, plus more for frying

1 teaspoon minced fresh ginger

1 tablespoon minced garlic

1 teaspoon cumin seeds, toasted

1 teaspoon paprika

1 teaspoon ground coriander

½ teaspoon mustard seeds

½ teaspoon fennel seeds

sea salt

cayenne pepper

1 teaspoon amchur or vinegar

1½ cups julienned onion

1 cup chickpea flour

½ cup rice flour

2 teaspoons black cumin seeds

1½ cups beer or soda water

1 quart buttermilk

2 sprigs fresh sage

1 small onion, peeled and studded with 6 cloves

pinch of nutmeg

2 pounds heritage turkey breast, cut into 1-inch-thick slices

In a large sauté pan over high heat, cook the eggplant in the oil until lightly browned, about 4 minutes. Reduce the heat to medium, add the ginger and garlic and cook until just beginning to color. Add the spices and cook for 2 minutes, until aromatic. Pour in ½ cup water and cook until reduced by half. Season with salt, cayenne pepper, and the amchur or vinegar.

In a large saucepan, heat 2 inches oil to 375°F, as measured by a deep-fry thermometer. In a medium bowl, mix together the julienned onion, chickpea flour, rice flour, and black cumin seeds. Pour in the beer until the batter has the consistency of pancake batter. Season with salt and stir well. Using a tablespoon, drop spoonfuls of batter into the hot oil and fry until golden on the outside and firm in the center. Using a handheld strainer, transfer the onion beignets to paper towels to drain. Continue until the batter is used up.

In a medium pot over medium heat, combine the buttermilk, sage, clove-studded onion and nutmeg. Cook until the milk begins to simmer, about 5 minutes. Reduce the heat to maintain a simmer. Season the turkey with salt and cook in the simmering buttermilk for 10 minutes, until it reaches 155°F on an instant-read thermometer or is firm to the touch and cooked through. Remove the pot from the heat and let stand for 5 minutes.

Divide the turkey among four warmed plates. Garnish each with the eggplant curry and onion beignets. Serve immediately.

CHICKEN & PUMPKIN BRAISED IN GREEN CURRY WITH PRESSED RICOTTA

Sweet pumpkin and zesty, made-from-scratch green curry are a great combination. The soft poached chicken shows well here against the other flavors. Inspired by the Indian farmer's cheese known as paneer, I've made a homemade pressed ricotta, which needs to be prepared a day ahead.

SERVES 4

4 cups winter squash or pumpkin, peeled and sliced into rounds
3 tablespoons sunflower oil
sea salt
½ cup diced onion
4 tablespoons minced fresh ginger
2 cups chicken stock (see larder)
4 cups coconut milk
4 chicken breasts
1 cup fresh chopped cilantro, plus 4 sprigs for garnish
1 cup chopped spinach
1 cup chopped mizuna
2 green chiles, such as jalapeños, deseeded
¼ cup garlic cloves
2 fresh lime leaves
1 tablespoon dried shrimp
lemon juice

RICOTTA CHEESE

1 quart whole milk
2 tablespoon lemon juice
2 tablespoons heavy cream
sea salt

First, make the ricotta: In a medium pot over high heat, heat the milk until its temperature reaches 145°F on a candy thermometer. Remove the pot from the heat and, while stirring, add the lemon juice. Let the milk stand for 10 minutes, then separate the curds from the whey and transfer to a small bowl. If the curds do not fully separate, return the pot to the heat until they separate. Stir in the cream and season with salt. Wrap the curds in cheesecloth, forming a ball. Place in a bowl and let drain in the refrigerator overnight.

Preheat the oven to 450°F. In a medium bowl, toss the pumpkin with 2 tablespoons of the oil. Season with salt and spread the pumpkin on a baking sheet in a single layer. Bake until tender and beginning to brown, about 10 minutes. Remove from the oven to cool.

In a medium pot over high heat, sauté half of the onions and half of the ginger in the remaining 1 tablespoon oil until the onion just begins to color, about 3 minutes. Pour in the stock and 2 cups of the coconut milk and bring to a boil. Reduce the heat to low. Season the chicken breasts with salt and add to the pot. Poach the chicken until firm to the touch and cooked through. Remove the pot from the heat and let stand 5 minutes.

In the bowl of a food processor, combine the cilantro, spinach, mizuna, chiles, remaining 2 tablespoons ginger, remaining ¼ cup onion, the garlic, lime leaves and dried shrimp. Process until the mixture forms a paste, then transfer to a medium pot over low heat. Stir in the remaining 2 cups coconut milk. Heat gently until warmed through. Season with salt and lemon juice to taste.

Form the ricotta cheese into 8 equal pieces. Add the cheese and the pumpkin to the curry and heat gently until warmed through. Add the poached chicken.

Divide the curry among four large bowls. Garnish with the cilantro sprigs and serve immediately.

ROASTED DUCK DUCK CONFIT SPRING ROLLS

Redolent with aromatic spices, this duck dish is a favorite of mine—it's satisfying in the winter, but not too heavy or sweet as many duck dishes can be. Chinese five-spice is a unique spice blend composed of cinnamon, Szechuan pepper, clove, star anise and fennel. Here, it combines with fresh and candied citrus to create wonderful winter spice notes that perfume the duck. Additions of sesame ground the dish, and the mustard flowers add a bright touch.

SERVES 4

2 duck confit legs (see larder)
2 Satsuma oranges
1 tablespoon sunflower oil
2 tablespoons sesame oil
1 medium onion, julienned
2 tablespoons minced garlic
1 tablespoon minced fresh
    ginger
1 cup julienned napa cabbage
1 tablespoon Chinese
    five-spice powder
sea salt
1 tablespoon lemon juice
4 spring roll wrappers
2 cups duck stock (see larder)
4 duck breasts, trimmed and
    scored
1 cup mizuna leaves
1 cup mustard flowers

Preheat the oven to 400°F. Separate the duck confit meat from the legs and discard the bones. Break the meat up into coarse chunks and set aside.

Remove 3 tablespoons zest from the oranges. Peel and slice; squeeze ¼ cup orange juice from one orange and peel and slice the second orange.

In a large sauté pan over high heat, combine the sunflower oil, 1 tablespoon of the sesame oil, the onion, garlic, ginger and cabbage and cook, stirring often, until the vegetables are just beginning to color, about 6 minutes. Add the duck meat, 2 tablespoons of the orange zest and the five-spice powder and cook for 3 minutes. Remove the pan from the heat, season with salt and the lemon juice and let cool.

On a work surface, lay out the spring roll wrappers individually. Divide the cabbage mixture between the wrappers. Tightly roll up, tucking in the sides. Place the rolls on a baking sheet, seam side down, and bake until crisp and golden, about 8 minutes. Remove from the oven and keep warm.

In a medium saucepan over high heat, combine the stock, the remaining 1 tablespoon orange zest, the orange juice and the remaining 1 tablespoon sesame oil. Boil until reduced by half. Season with salt and keep warm.

Season the duck with salt on both sides. In a stainless-steel sauté pan over medium-low heat, gently cook the duck, skin side down, pouring off the rendered fat occasionally, until the fat is fully rendered and the skin becomes crisp, about 20 minutes. Turn the breasts over and cook until they firm up and are pink in the middle, about 3 minutes more. Remove the breasts from the pan to a warm place to rest for 5 minutes, then slice crosswise very thinly.

Cut the spring rolls in half and divide among four warmed plates. Place the duck breasts alongside the spring rolls. Garnish with mizuna leaves, orange slices and mustard flowers and drizzle with the reduced stock. Serve immediately.

BRINED TURKEY
WITH APPLE, TARRAGON & CELERY ROOT

Every year at the Black Cat we serve a traditional Thanksgiving dinner. It is my chance to cook all of the dishes I remember from my childhood. This turkey dish is inspired by a wonderful recipe of my mom's she made every year when she pulled out all the stops.

SERVES 4

BRINE

1 cup salt

½ cup brown sugar

2 lemons, quartered

6 sprigs fresh thyme

4 bay leaves

1 tablespoon juniper berries

1 tablespoon black
   peppercorns

1 whole heritage turkey, about
   12 pounds

6 tablespoons unsalted butter,
   softened

4 tablespoons minced
   lemon zest

4 cloves garlic, minced

4 tablespoons minced fresh
   tarragon

1 medium onion, diced

¼ cup minced garlic

2 cups diced celery root

2 cups peeled and diced
   apples

3 cups diced wheat bread

2 cups turkey stock, plus more
   for basting (see larder)

sea salt and freshly ground
   black pepper

To make the brine, dissolve the salt and brown sugar in 2 gallons of cold water in a nonreactive container (such as a clean bucket or large stockpot, or a clean, heavy-duty plastic garbage bag). Add the lemons, thyme, bay leaves, juniper and black peppercorns.

Rinse the turkey inside and out under cold running water, then soak in the brine, covered and refrigerated, for at least 4 hours and up to 24.

The next day, preheat the oven to 325°F. Remove the turkey from the brine and rinse well under cold running water. Pat dry with paper towels and place in a large roasting pan. Roast the turkey for 1 hour.

Meanwhile, in a food processor, combine 3 tablespoons butter, 2 tablespoons lemon zest, the garlic, and 2 tablespoons tarragon. Process to form a paste and set aside.

Remove the turkey from the oven and baste with pan juices or the stock. Rub the turkey all over with the lemon butter. Return to the oven and roast, basting every hour, until an instant-read thermometer registers 165°F when inserted into the largest section of thigh (avoiding the bone), 2¾ to 3 hours total cooking time.

Before the last hour of roasting the turkey, make the stuffing: In a saucepan over high heat, combine the onion, garlic, celery root and the remaining 3 tablespoons butter and cook until the onion begins to brown, about 6 minutes. Add the apples and cook for 5 minutes more. Transfer to a large bowl and mix in the bread, stock, and the remaining tarragon and lemon zest. Season with salt and pepper and toss well. Transfer the stuffing to a large baking dish and bake until golden, about 45 minutes.

Transfer the turkey to a platter and let rest for 20 minutes before carving. Carve and serve the turkey with the stuffing on the side.

SAUTÉED HERITAGE TURKEY
WITH PROSCIUTTO, SAGE & CHANTERELLES

Taking a cue from the classic Italian dish Saltimbocca, this dish is a quick alternative to a whole roasted bird. The slices of breast cook up quickly and stay very tender. I love to feature our heritage turkeys and our handmade dried hams this way.

SERVES 4

2 pounds heritage turkey, cut into ½-inch-thick slices

sea salt and freshly ground black pepper

2 tablespoons sunflower oil

2 medium onions, julienned

3 cups sliced chanterelle mushrooms (see note)

2 tablespoons unsalted butter, softened

2 tablespoons white wine

3 sprigs fresh sage

1 cup thinly sliced prosciutto or dried ham

Season the turkey on one side with salt and pepper. In a large sauté pan over high heat, sauté the turkey in the oil until lightly browned, about 3 minutes. Turn the turkey slices and cook 1 minute more. Transfer to a platter to rest.

Return the sauté pan to the heat. Add the onions, mushrooms and butter. Cook until the onions just begin to brown, about 5 minutes. Deglaze the pan with the wine, scraping to loosen any stuck bits. Add the sage and prosciutto and cook for 2 minutes. Season with salt.

Divide the turkey slices among four warmed plates. Top each with the onions, mushrooms and prosciutto and serve immediately.

CHANTERELLES
Summer afternoons after our farmer's market booth closes, I drive with my family into the high mountains above our farm to forage mushrooms. It is my chance to relax after a hectic week. For my kids, mushroom foraging is a great treasure hunt. It's very fitting that the chanterelles we seek are such a brilliant gold. They are a great foraging mushroom due to their easy identification; there are no poisonous look-alikes to worry about. At different parts of the summer the mushroom varieties we find change from morels early on, into porcinis, then finally to the chanterelles. Foraging with the family is a perfect time. It combines relaxation, togetherness, aimless wandering, nature and, of course, golden treasure. If our foraging trip has been rained out, I opt for cultivated mushrooms like shiitakes, oysters or cinnamon caps.

PORK

THE OLD FARMER'S SAYING, "EVERYTHING BUT THE SQUEAK," IS VERY
APPROPRIATE FOR WHICH PARTS OF THE PIG TO USE. FROM NOSE TO TAIL,
IT'S EASY TO FIND DELICIOUS USES FOR THE WHOLE HOG. TAKE THE TIME TO
SEARCH FOR PASTURE-RAISED HERITAGE BREED PIGS. THE RESULTS IN THE
KITCHEN ARE WORTH EVERY BIT OF THE EFFORT.

PORK CONFIT
WITH GINGER GASTRIQUE

I like to add warm spices like cinnamon or cardamom to pork as it slowly cooks. The result is succulent meat whose perfume is haunting. The sweet-sour gastrique is a typical accompaniment to slow-cooked pork confit as the sauce can stand up to the rich meat. Ginger adds a touch of spark and is a good match for fresh cherries.

SERVES 4

2 pounds pork shoulder
sea salt
1 quart plus 2 tablespoons pork fat
1 orange, halved
1 cinnamon stick
2 pieces star anise
4 cardamom pods
2 cups white vinegar
1 cup sugar
2 tablespoons very thinly sliced fresh ginger
1 pound asparagus, peeled
lemon juice to taste
1½ cups fresh cherries, pitted

Preheat the oven to 200°F. Season the pork with salt.

In a heavy-bottomed braising pan over medium heat, combine the pork, 1 quart of the fat, the orange and spices. Cook until the fat is melted and begins to simmer, about 10 minutes. Transfer the braising pan to the oven and cook until the pork is very tender, about 4 hours. Remove from the oven to a warm place.

Meanwhile, in a small pot over high heat, combine the vinegar, sugar and ginger. Cook until the mixture begins to thicken, about 45 minutes.

In a large sauté pan over high heat, combine the asparagus with the remaining 2 tablespoons pork fat. Cook until just tender, about 3 minutes. Season with salt and lemon juice.

Divide the asparagus among four plates. Top with the pork, its sauce and the cherries. Serve immediately.

POACHED HAM
WITH SAUCE GRIBICHE

One of my favorite ways to serve boiled ham is in this delicious terrine, perfect for a light lunch. The rosy ham is set off by the fresh flavor of chervil, a delicate anise-flavored herb. Gribiche is a traditional sauce made of hard-boiled egg, herbs and aïoli.

SERVES 6

1½ cups chopped fresh chervil
2 ice cubes
3 tablespoons sunflower oil, plus more for greasing
1 cup pork or chicken stock (see larder)
2 sheets gelatin, soaked in cold water
lemon juice to taste
sea salt
1½ pounds boiled ham, cut into ¼-inch slices

SAUCE GRIBICHE
2 hard-boiled eggs, peeled and diced
2 tablespoons chopped fresh chervil
1 tablespoon chopped fresh tarragon
1 tablespoon chopped fresh parsley
1 tablespoon minced shallots
1 tablespoon drained and minced capers
2 cups traditional aïoli (see larder)

In a blender, purée the chervil, ice cubes and oil until very smooth, about 2 minutes. In a small saucepan over medium heat, warm the stock. Off the heat, add the gelatin, season with lemon juice and a pinch of salt and mix well. Stir in the chervil purée.

Lightly oil the inside of a loaf pan and line with plastic wrap. Loosely layer the ham slices in the pan, alternating with the chervil purée. Continue until the ham and purée are all used up. Place in the refrigerator to thoroughly chill, about 3 hours.

When you are ready to serve the terrine, make the sauce gribiche: In a small bowl, combine the eggs, herbs, shallots, capers and aïoli. Season with lemon juice and salt and mix well.

Slice the terrine and serve with the sauce gribiche on the side.

PORK ROAST WITH FERMENTED BLACK BEANS & BAY SCALLOPS

Pork and seafood are a great combination as their flavors build off of each other. Here, I've used them in a dish straddling the French-Chinese cuisine line. Young green garlic and gai lan, or Chinese broccoli, are stewed in butter and finished with tender bay scallops. Fermented black beans add a subtle umami layer that ties the dish together. The combination of flavors is like a symphony. It is stunning.

SERVES 4

¼ cup fermented black beans
pinch of ground clove
pinch of ground cardamom
1 teaspoon ground coriander
1 tablespoon chopped young
   garlic, plus ½ cup thinly
   sliced
2 pounds pork loin
sea salt and freshly ground
   black pepper
2 cups gai lan or rapini
1 tablespoon julienned fresh
   ginger
¼ cup unsalted butter,
   softened
1 cup bay scallops, rinsed
rice wine vinegar

In a small pot over high heat, combine ½ cup water with the black beans, spices and chopped garlic. Boil until reduced by three-quarters. Transfer to a blender and purée until smooth. Set aside.

Season the pork with salt and pepper. In a large sauté pan over high heat, sauté the pork loin, fat side down, until browned and crisp, about 7 minutes. Drain the rendered fat from the pan and save for another use.

Turn the pork over and cook until browned, about 10 minutes more. Reduce the temperature to low and cook until the interior of the loin is cooked but still rosy, about 5 minutes more. Transfer to a clean platter to rest for 10 minutes.

Return the sauté pan with the pan drippings to the heat and add the gai lan, sliced garlic and ginger. Cook until the gai lan begins to wilt, then add the butter and cook for 1 minute more. Remove the pan from the heat and add the scallops. Season with salt and vinegar; the scallops will warm through as the pan cools.

Thinly slice the pork crosswise and divide among four dinner plates. Top with the black bean purée and garnish with the gai lan mixture. Serve immediately.

*Overleaf: Grilled pork steak
with borlotti bean salad and
Heirloom borlotti beans*

GRILLED PORK STEAK WITH BORLOTTI BEAN SALAD

At the farmer's market, in the heat of the summer, I often recommend this dish as a way to best enjoy our heritage pork with a minimum of fuss and time spent in the kitchen. The components are served chilled, which makes for a simple, casual meal. Sauce verte is a simple herb and olive oil purée that livens up almost any dish.

SERVES 4

3 cups fresh borlotti beans, shelled (see note)

¼ cup finely diced onion

2 teaspoons minced garlic plus 1 clove garlic, minced

¼ cup finely diced carrot

1 sprig fresh rosemary

2 fresh bay leaves

2 tablespoons fresh parsley leaves

¼ cup basic vinaigrette (see larder)

sea salt and freshly ground black pepper

4 heirloom tomatoes, sliced

3 tablespoons olive oil

1 tablespoon red wine vinegar

4 sprigs fresh thyme

2 pounds ham steaks

SAUCE VERTE

¼ cup fresh parsley leaves

¼ cup chopped fresh basil

2 tablespoons fresh tarragon leaves

½ cup chopped mustard greens

½ cup chopped arugula

2 scallions, chopped

2 tablespoons lemon zest

¼ cup capers

½ cup olive oil

sea salt

lemon juice

In a medium saucepan over high heat, combine the beans, onion, 2 teaspoons of the minced garlic, carrot, rosemary and bay leaves with 1½ cups water. Boil until the water has evaporated, about 5 minutes. Transfer to a medium bowl and toss with the parsley and vinaigrette. Season with salt and pepper and mix well.

Make the sauce verte: In the bowl of a food processor, combine the herbs, greens, scallions, lemon zest, capers and olive oil. Process until finely ground, about 30 seconds. Season with salt and lemon juice and set aside.

In a medium bowl, combine the tomatoes, oil, vinegar, the remaining 1 clove minced garlic and thyme.

Season the ham steaks with salt and place fat side down in a large ovenproof sauté pan over medium-high heat. Render the fat until crispy and golden, about 10 minutes. Turn the steaks to brown on the second side, about 10 minutes more, until the internal temperature of the steaks reaches 134°F, as measured by a meat thermometer. Transfer the steaks to a platter and season with pepper.

Spread a thin layer of sauce verte on four dinner plates. Place a ham steak atop the sauce. Top each steak with the bean and tomato salads. Serve immediately.

HEIRLOOM BEANS

We use a variety of beans at the restaurant: hutterite, scarlett runner, borlotti, rattlesnake, and others. I look for different colors, shapes and textures—the broader the range the better. Soaking the beans in water overnight evens out the disparate cooking times one finds when using a variety of dry beans in one recipe. Or, better yet, ask your local farmer to harvest some fresh shell beans for you. These are the same beans harvested before they dry down and harden—and they are a delight. Cooked in minutes rather than hours, they taste much, much better. Unfortunately, their September season is short, so enjoy this treat while you can.

PORCHETTA WITH SEMOLINA DUMPLINGS

Porchetta is a masterpiece. Pork loin wrapped in pork belly, roasted whole and scented with rosemary. While it takes a bit of work and a day or two to air dry, the results are spectacular. I've paired the pork with simple but delicious accompaniments. Grilled cardoons, a close cousin to the artichoke, lend a fresh, yet smoky note. The semolina dumplings are a more toothsome version of gnocchi that can stand up to the meaty pork.

SERVES 4 TO 6

1 pork loin with skin on, belly attached, or 1 pork loin and 1 piece pork belly (about 3 pounds)

sea salt and freshly ground black pepper

3 tablespoons minced garlic

3 tablespoons minced fresh parsley

3 tablespoons minced fresh rosemary

3 tablespoons julienned lemon zest

6 large cardoon stalks, peeled and cut into 4-inch lengths

3 tablespoons lemon juice

2 tablespoons sunflower oil

3 cups semolina flour

2 cups pork stock (see larder)

4 bay leaves

6 egg yolks

olive oil for finishing

On a clean work surface, place the pork loin and belly, skin side down. Using a knife, score the belly flesh in a diamond pattern ⅓ inch deep. Season with salt and pepper, then rub the belly and loin with the garlic, parsley, 1 tablespoon of the rosemary and the zest. Tightly roll the pork and secure, using loops of butcher's twine. Using a sharp knife, poke the pork skin, once about every inch, across the surface of the roast. Transfer to a wire rack set on a baking sheet.

Air-dry the roast in the refrigerator, uncovered, for 1 to 2 days. Dry the skin with paper towels occasionally if moisture comes to the surface.

Remove the porchetta from the refrigerator 2 hours prior to roasting. Preheat the oven to 500°F.

Roast the pork until lightly browned, about 1 hour, turning once. Reduce the oven temperature to 250°F and roast until the pork is browned and the internal temperature reaches 140°F, about 2 hours more. Remove the pork from the oven and let rest for 20 minutes.

In a medium pot over high heat, combine the cardoons and lemon juice. Add enough water to cover and season with salt. Cook until tender, about 40 minutes. Drain the cardoons in a colander, then toss with the oil. Grill the cardoons over a wood or charcoal flame until lightly charred, about 3 minutes. Or broil the cardoons in the oven until browned. Set aside.

In a small pot over medium-high heat, combine the flour, 2 cups cold water, the stock and bay leaves. Cook, stirring constantly, until the mixture is very thick and has a glassy appearance, about 20 minutes. Transfer the flour to a medium bowl and mix well with the egg yolks and remaining 2 tablespoons rosemary.

Heat a large pot of salted water to a boil. Transfer the dough to a lightly floured work surface and form it into long logs, about ¾ inch in diameter. Cut the logs crosswise into ¾-inch pieces. Boil until the dumplings are firm, about 5 minutes. Strain in a colander and transfer to a medium bowl. Toss well with the cardoons and olive oil.

Cut the porchetta into thin slices. Divide among four to six dinner plates. Top each with the dumplings and cardoons and serve immediately.

SMOKED PORK WITH PORK NOODLES & BABY CORN

Here is a full-throttle dish for those pork-o-philes out there. It combines brined and then smoked pork shoulder with al dente "pork noodles" made of braised pork skin. Hon tsai tai is a purple Chinese broccoli rabe that balances sweetness with a robust flavor.

SERVES 4

sea salt

2 tablespoons sugar

2 tablespoons freshly ground pepper

2 pounds pork shoulder

1 medium onion, diced, plus ¼ cup julienned onion

1 quart plus ½ cup pork or chicken stock (see larder)

6 cloves garlic, minced, plus 2 tablespoons

3 tablespoons sliced fresh ginger

3 tablespoons Thai chili sauce

1 pound pork skin, cleaned of all fat (ask your local butcher)

one 7-inch piece kombu

4 bay leaves

1 teaspoon freshly grated nutmeg

¼ cup plus 2 tablespoons rice vinegar

2 tablespoons julienned pickled ginger (see larder)

12 ears baby corn, cut into 1-inch pieces

2 cups hon tsai tai, chopped

2 tablespoons sunflower oil

Preheat the oven to 200°F.

In a medium bowl, place 1 cup salt, the sugar and pepper in 1 quart warm water and stir until the salt and sugar dissolve. Fully cool in the refrigerator, about 1 hour, and then add the pork and marinate in the refrigerator for 6 hours.

Remove the pork from the brine and dry with paper towels. Place the pork and the diced onion in a heavy braising pan and cook until the pork is browned on all sides, about 4 minutes per side. Add the stock, 6 cloves minced garlic, 1 tablespoon of the ginger and 2 tablespoons of the chili sauce and bring to a boil. Cover and place the pan in the oven and braise until the pork is fall-apart tender, about 6 hours.

In a pressure cooker, combine the pork skin, kombu, bay leaves, and remaining 2 tablespoons ginger. Add enough water to cover and season with salt. Cook until the skin is very tender, about 30 minutes. Cool the pressure cooker and place the pork skin on a cutting board to cool. When cool enough to handle, roll the skin into a tight spiral. Thinly slice crosswise to form thin strips or "noodles." Transfer to a bowl and toss with the nutmeg, julienned onion, ¼ cup of the rice vinegar, and the pickled ginger. Season with salt and set aside.

In a large sauté pan over high heat, sauté the remaining 2 tablespoons garlic, the corn, hon tsai tai and oil until the greens begin to wilt, about 1 minute. Mix in the pork noodles, remaining ½ cup stock, 2 tablespoons rice vinegar and 1 tablespoon chili sauce and cook until the noodles are just heated through and the broth is hot.

Divide the noodles among four large bowls. Top each with some of the pork and serve immediately.

CHINESE BARBECUE PORK WITH MELON

Last summer, we had bumper crops of Asian cucumbers and cilantro. I combined them with an Asian vinaigrette for a quick, refreshing and delicious salad that became the starting point for this dish. As I am a big fan of the Chinese dish, twice-cooked pork, I decided to combine it with the salad to create a fun summer entrée. I use slow-braised pork shoulder here, rubbed with spices and sweet soy sauce, which is soy sauce thickened with palm sugar and spices.

SERVES 4

2 pounds pork shoulder

sea salt

2 tablespoons minced fresh ginger

1 medium onion, julienned

2 tablespoons minced garlic

2 large carrots, sliced

1½ quarts pork stock or water

2 tablespoons paprika

2 tablespoons ground coriander

1 tablespoon black pepper

2 teaspoons fennel seeds

1 teaspoon ground cinnamon

1 teaspoon cayenne pepper

1 teaspoon ground cardamom

1 cup brown sugar

¼ cup plus 1 tablespoon sesame oil

1 cup plus 1 tablespoon rice vinegar

1 cup sweet soy sauce

¼ cup hoisin sauce

2 cucumbers, peeled and deseeded

2 cups sliced melon

3 cups fresh cilantro, large stems removed

1 tablespoon sunflower oil

1 tablespoon pickled ginger, julienned (see larder)

Preheat the oven to 200°F.

Season the pork with salt. Place in a heavy braising pan over high heat with the ginger, onion, garlic, carrots and stock and bring to a boil for about 7 minutes. Place the pan in the oven and braise, covered, until the pork is very tender, about 6 hours. Transfer the pork to a mixing bowl. (Strain the remaining pork broth through a fine sieve, discarding the solids, and save for another use.) Add the spices, brown sugar, ¼ cup of the sesame oil, 1 cup of the vinegar, the sweet soy sauce and hoisin sauce. Dress the pork well and marinate while preparing the salad.

Using a mandolin, very thinly slice the cucumber. Place in a medium bowl and add the melon, cilantro, sunflower oil, the remaining 1 tablespoon each of sesame oil and vinegar and the pickled ginger. Season with salt and toss well.

Divide the pork among four dinner plates. Top with the cucumber salad and serve immediately.

ROASTED HAM
WITH GRILLED LEMONS & PLUMS

I wait until after the first frost to harvest Treviso for this dish, as it's not until after the frosts that this chicory's bitterness is replaced by a delicate sweetness. Warmed gently in the drippings from the roasting ham, its flavor is otherworldly.

SERVES 4

2 pounds fresh ham
sea salt
1 tablespoon ground
   juniper
1 teaspoon ground
   allspice

3 cups radicchio di
   Treviso
6 plums, halved
1 lemon, very thinly sliced
2 tablespoons sunflower
   oil

Preheat the oven to 450°F.

Season the ham with salt, the juniper and allspice. Score the fat in a 1-inch diamond pattern. In a heavy-bottomed roasting pan over high heat, cook the ham, fat side down, until browned and crispy. Turn the roast over and place the pan in the oven. Roast until the internal temperature reaches 140°F, about 1 hour. Transfer the ham to a platter to rest.

Pour out all but 3 tablespoons of the fat from the roasting pan. Place on the stovetop over low heat. Add the Treviso and cook until wilted, about 1 minute. Season with salt.

Toss the plums and lemon slices in the oil and season with salt. Grill over a wood or charcoal fire until lightly charred and warmed through, about 4 minutes.

Thinly slice the ham and divide among four dinner plates. Top with the Treviso and the grilled lemons and plums. Serve immediately.

GRILLED PORK CHOPS
WITH HUNTER'S SAUCE

Our heritage Mulefoot pork needs little accompaniment. Here, I've added only a quick sauce and a simple purée of parsnips. The sauce captures the essence of fall and includes ingredients that a hunter may have during the hunt—some wild mushrooms, dried ham, herbs and a touch of wine.

SERVES 4

1 pound parsnips,
   trimmed
1 medium russet potato
sea salt
½ cup heavy cream
4 slices smoked bacon,
   diced
1 medium onion, julienned
2 tablespoons minced
   garlic
1 pound wild mushrooms,
   chopped

2 cups red wine
2 cups pork stock
   (see larder)
1 sprig fresh rosemary
1 tablespoon crushed
   juniper berries
½ cup julienned dried
   ham, such as prosciutto
3 tablespoons unsalted
   butter, softened
4 pork chops
freshly ground black
   pepper

In a medium saucepan over high heat, cover the parsnips and potato with lightly salted water. Cook until the potato is very tender, about 30 minutes. Using a hand whisk, mash until very smooth. Add the cream and season with salt.

In a large saucepan over high heat, cook the bacon, onion, garlic and mushrooms until the onion is browned, about 10 minutes. Add the wine, stock, rosemary and juniper and cook until thickened, about 30 minutes. Remove from the heat, stir in the ham and butter, season with salt and keep warm.

Season the pork with salt. Grill over a wood or charcoal fire, turning often, for about 12 minutes. Transfer to a platter, season with pepper and let rest.

Divide the pork among four plates. Add a scoop of the parsnip purée and top with the sauce.

AUTUMN ON THE FARM

Thinking about fall harvests, I am humbled by the bounty of our farm. The tail end of summer vegetables is still with us as the nights turn chilly. Then along come the fall vegetables: pumpkins, fall roots, cabbages and greens. In autumn, there is always much more than we can use. The hours spent in the fields are replaced with hours behind the stove putting up the harvest for winter. Giant pots of tomato sauce, vats of homemade pickles and sauerkraut, brandied fruits, and apple butter are just some of the regulars added to the fall larder. Deep in the fall, when the last of the warmth has left the air, we begin to fill the giant root cellars under the farm. By the beginning of December, the harvest is in and safely tucked away. The farm has been put to bed.

PUMPKINS

The Black Cat Farm pumpkin patch extends over 5 acres and includes a selection of fourteen varieties. All winter squashes or pumpkins (there is no botanical separation between the two) fall into three types: pepo, maxima and moschata, each with its own unique qualities. The pepos include the small acorns and delicata squashes that are perfect for roasting and then stuffing. The flesh of the maxima group is drier, denser, and packed with flavor. These make the best soups and purées. While the thin-skinned moschatas, like butternut and tromboncino, excel when peeling and dicing is necessary. Growing winter squashes at home is easy, especially if you have the space to let the vines run across the yard. And run they will!

SPICED PORK TENDERLOIN
WITH SMOKED EGGPLANT, YOGURT & POMEGRANATE

I enjoy serving this elegant, yet exotic entrée in the winter. The eggplant purée is a variation on *babaganouj*, smoky and delicious. Each fall we grill and smoke mountains of eggplant to make this purée. It freezes well and is very versatile; use it also on the grilled lamb with fattoush and petrale sole with summer vegetables (pages 136 and 175).

SERVES 4

1 large eggplant
½ cup roasted garlic
    (see larder)
2 tablespoons sesame oil
2 tablespoons olive oil
sea salt
lemon juice to taste
2 cups plain yogurt
1 tablespoon honey
2 teaspoons ground
    cardamom
2 pounds pork tenderloin
1 tablespoon pork fat or butter
1 tablespoon ground dried
    orange peel
1 teaspoon ground grains of
    paradise (see note)
2 tablespoons pomegranate
    molasses
3 tablespoons fresh
    pomegranate seeds

Over a wood or charcoal fire or an open flame on the stovetop, grill the eggplant until the skin is fully charred. Transfer to a bowl and cover tightly with plastic wrap. The eggplant will steam in the bowl as it cools and the skin will loosen. Once cool, peel the eggplant. Rinse under lightly running water, if necessary, to remove the charred bits.

Transfer to a blender. Add the roasted garlic and both oils and purée until smooth, about 2 minutes. Season with salt and lemon juice and set aside.

In a small bowl, combine the yogurt, honey and 1 teaspoon of the cardamom. Season with salt, mix well and set aside.

Season the pork with salt. In a large sauté pan over high heat, sauté in the pork fat until golden. Transfer to a platter to rest.

Pour off the fat from the pan. Return the pan to the stove over low heat. Add the orange peel, remaining 1 teaspoon cardamom, and the grains of paradise and cook for 1 minute. Stir in 2 tablespoons water and the pomegranate molasses, scraping the browned bits from the pan. When the sauce has thickened slightly, remove the pan from the heat.

Cut the pork into 2-inch pieces and divide among four plates. Garnish with the eggplant purée and the honey yogurt. Top the meat with the pomegranate sauce and pomegranate seeds and serve immediately.

GRAINS OF PARADISE
A West African spice, grains of paradise adds a heat to dishes that's similar to pepper but with a floral-cardamom note. An easy way to add an exotic touch to grilled meats and vegetables, it should be added only at the end of cooking, as its flavor dissipates quickly with heat.

PORK SHOULDER SMOKED OVER PLUM WOOD

In the cold heart of winter, our restaurant's forager, Colin, begins the arduous task of pruning fruit trees to prepare them for the coming spring. Loads of branch trimmings make their way to the farm. We cut them into manageable pieces to use in our smoker, which is when I begin to serve this dish. The pork is brined to add depth of flavor and to boost its juiciness, then cold-smoked for a few hours before a slow, low roast achieves perfect tenderness. I top it with vadouvan, an Indian spice blend that adds an exotic yet comforting touch.

SERVES 4

sea salt
1 tablespoon freshly ground black pepper
1 tablespoon ground fennel seeds
1 tablespoon ground cardamom
2 pounds pork shoulder
2 large carrots, trimmed
2 parsnips, trimmed
4 parsley roots, trimmed
4 fingerling potatoes
dash of olive oil

VADOUVAN

2 tablespoons sunflower oil
½ cup diced onions
¼ cup diced leeks
2 teaspoons minced garlic
1 tablespoon ground cumin
1 tablespoon ground coriander
1 tablespoon ground fennel
1 tablespoon mustard seeds
1 teaspoon black cumin seeds
1 teaspoon ground fenugreek
1 teaspoon ground nutmeg
½ teaspoon ground cloves
lemon juice to taste

In a large stockpot over high heat, boil 2 quarts of water with 2 tablespoons salt, the pepper, fennel seeds and cardamom for 2 minutes. Let cool completely. Combine the pork shoulder and the brine in a suitably sized container and marinate in the refrigerator for 4 hours or overnight.

Remove the pork from the brine. Cold smoke for 3 hours over plum wood (see tip). Preheat the oven to 200°F.

Transfer the smoked pork to a roasting pan and roast in the oven until very tender, about 3 hours.

Meanwhile, nestle the root vegetables in the plum wood coals of the smoker and cook until charred and just tender, about 40 minutes. Remove the roots and peel, wiping with a damp towel. Cut into large chunks, dress in the olive oil and season with salt. Keep warm.

To make the vadouvan, in a large sauté pan over medium heat, combine the sunflower oil, onions and leeks and cook until the onions are translucent, about 5 minutes. Add the garlic and all of the spices and cook until very aromatic, about 5 minutes more. Season with salt and lemon juice.

Thinly slice the pork and divide among four dinner plates. Top with the vadouvan and garnish with the smoked roots. Serve immediately.

COOKING TIP

There are two methods of smoking foods: hot or cold. Hot smoking is easier and faster as it combines the smoking and cooking processes. The smoke and fire are very hot, about 400°F. With cold smoking, the two processes are separate. First, the food is smoked with smoke that is rather cool, about 70°F; then it's cooked. While cold smoking is more difficult, it has the advantage of a longer smoking time, which fully develops flavor. Additionally, there is no risk of drying the meat out with too much heat as it smokes. For the home cook, ice comes in handy for cooling the smoke in a smoker. Packing ice cubes around the meat or, better yet, forcing the smoke to pass through a layer of ice on its way to the meat are easy ways to produce this effect.

SLOW-COOKED PORK SHANKS
WITH HEIRLOOM BEANS

Inspired by the classic cassoulet, this pork version shares many qualities, including long, slow, gentle cooking that yields pork of a velvety texture. The bacon adds a smoky background touch that is perfect on a bracingly cold night. In the heart of the winter, when the farm is asleep under a blanket of snow, the challenge of keeping the restaurant supplied becomes our major focus. One of the solutions is to look back to how dishes were made more than one hundred years ago. Cassoulet is just such a dish.

SERVES 4

2 cups heirloom beans
   (see note, page 114)
sea salt
6 slices smoked bacon, diced
1 large onion, diced
2 carrots, diced
4 ribs celery, diced
6 cloves garlic, peeled
4 pork shanks
1½ quarts pork stock
   (see larder)
4 bay leaves
2 cups red wine
freshly ground black pepper
traditional aïoli (see larder)

In a medium stockpot over high heat, cover the beans with water and bring to a boil. Immediately remove the pot from the heat, cover and soak the beans overnight.

Preheat the oven to 200°F.

Drain the soaked beans and return to the pot with fresh water to cover. Season with salt and boil the beans until they are just tender, about 1 hour. Strain the beans through a colander and set aside.

In a heavy-bottomed braising pan over high heat, combine the bacon, onion, carrots, celery and garlic. Cook, stirring frequently, until the onions begin to brown, about 8 minutes.

Season the shanks liberally with salt. Add the shanks, stock and bay leaves to the pot and bring to a boil. Transfer the pan to the oven and bake, covered, until the shanks are very tender, about 5 hours.

Remove the pan from the oven and gently fold in the beans and wine. Season with salt and pepper and bake for 30 minutes more.

Divide the shanks and beans among four dinner plates. Garnish with the aïoli and serve immediately.

LAMB & RABBIT

I'VE COME TO LOVE COOKING LAMB SHANKS AND SHOULDERS MOST. THEY MAKE FOR PERFECTLY BRAISED DISHES THAT TASTE WONDERFUL (AND ARE OFTEN THE EASIEST). OUR FARM NEIGHBOR PRODUCES THE RABBITS FOR OUR RESTAURANT AND IS THE SOURCE OF MANY PETER RABBIT JOKES. YOU CAN FIND RABBIT AT BUTCHER SHOPS, FARMER'S MARKETS OR SPECIAL ORDER FROM GROCERY STORES.

BRAISED RABBIT
WITH CURRY, PEAS & PEA VINES

The rich taste of rabbit pairs well with bold flavors like curry. Here, I've matched it with a traditional spring pea curry. It is a great combination. Often your butcher will offer rabbit legs for sale. Otherwise, buy whole rabbits and use the loins for the recipes on pages 138 or 145. Pea flowers and vines make a stunning visual on the plate and reinforce the freshness of the peas. Baby spinach or Asian greens like mizuna make a fine substitute.

SERVES 4

4 rabbit legs

2 tablespoons unsalted butter, softened

1 large onion, minced

2 tablespoons minced garlic

2 tablespoons curry powder (see larder)

2 cups rabbit or chicken stock (see tip), plus more as needed (see larder)

12 baby carrots

1 tablespoon tomato paste

2 cups shelled peas

2 tablespoons crème fraîche

sea salt

1 cup pea flowers and pea vines

In a heavy-bottomed braising pan over high heat, combine the rabbit, butter, onion and garlic and cook until the onions begin to color, about 5 minutes. Add the curry powder and cook until very aromatic, about 2 minutes more. Pour in the stock, reduce the heat to a simmer and cook until the rabbit is tender, about 2 hours. Add more stock or water, if necessary, to ensure the rabbit is covered with liquid.

Stir in the carrots and tomato paste and cook until the carrots are tender, about 4 minutes. Stir in the peas and crème fraiche. Remove from the heat and season with salt.

Divide the rabbit and curry among four warmed plates. Garnish with the pea flowers and pea vines. Serve immediately.

COOKING TIP

When making rabbit stock, I follow the same guidelines I use for any stock. First, I roast the bones to a mahogany hue before adding them to the pot to simmer with water. Roasting develops flavor. For rabbit and chicken stock, I add only enough water to cover the bones. Any extra water dilutes the flavor. Extracting flavor and aroma from bones takes longer than it does for vegetables. As a result, I start the bones simmering first and add the roasted vegetables halfway through cooking. Boiling stock, while quicker than simmering, makes it cloudy with emulsified fat and dulls the flavor. Resist the urge to boil your stock.

SLOW-COOKED LAMB SHOULDER
WITH MUSTARD SPÄTZLE & FAVA BEANS

I like to roast lamb shoulder in a heavy-bottomed roasting pan. After roasting, while the lamb is resting on the carving platter, I briefly toss endives and herbs into the hot lamb drippings. To me, endives cooked this way deserve to be presented in brown paper packages tied up with string as in that *Sound of Music* song.

SERVES 4

4 cups all-purpose flour
2 cups whole milk
2 large eggs
¼ cup plus 2 tablespoons whole-grain mustard
sea salt
2 cups fresh fava beans
2 tablespoons minced lemon zest
2 cups lamb or chicken stock
1 whole lamb shoulder, deboned
freshly ground black pepper
2 tablespoons fresh chervil, chopped
1 tablespoon fresh lovage, chopped
1 tablespoon fresh thyme leaves
3 cups endive leaves

Preheat the oven to 500°F.

In the bowl of an electric mixer, combine the flour, milk, eggs, ¼ cup of the mustard and 1 teaspoon salt. Mix on medium speed for 4 minutes or until the batter begins to become elastic. Over boiling salted water, pass the batter through a coarse colander or food mill so small pea-sized droplets drop into the water. Cook until the spätzle are al dente, about 4 minutes. Using a handheld strainer, transfer to a sheet tray to cool. Working in batches, continue cooking the spätzle until all the batter is gone.

In boiling salted water, blanch the fava beans briefly, about 20 seconds. Strain and, while still slightly warm, remove the inner bean by peeling the outer jacket and gently squeezing the bean to release. Continue until all the beans are cleaned and set aside.

In a medium saucepan over high heat, combine the lemon zest, remaining 2 tablespoons mustard and the stock. Boil until the stock is reduced by half, about 30 minutes. Season with salt and keep warm.

Place the lamb shoulder in a heavy-bottomed roasting pan and season with salt and pepper. Roast in the oven until the lamb begins to color, 10 to 12 minutes. Reduce the temperature to 190°F and roast until the lamb is very tender, about 4 hours. Remove from the oven and let rest for 10 minutes, then transfer to a carving board and slice thinly.

Return the roasting pan to the stovetop over low heat. Add the herbs and endive leaves, stirring well to combine. Cook until the leaves just begin to wilt, about 3 minutes. Season with salt.

Divide the lamb and endive mixture among four plates and top with the warm mustard sauce. Spoon some spätzle and fava beans alongside and serve immediately.

LAMB OSSOBUCO
WITH PARSLEY SALAD & POLENTA

I love this lamb version of the classic veal ossobuco. Like other braised dishes, it is a no-fuss dinner that tastes much better than the effort it takes to make. Taking a cue from the traditional accompaniment, a parsley-based gremolata, I've made a parsley salad that features roasted parsley roots as well as the leaves, adding a lightness to the dish.

SERVES 4

4 large lamb shanks, about 3 pounds total

sea salt

3 tablespoons sunflower oil

1 medium onion, quartered

4 cloves garlic, sliced

2 ribs celery, cut into 1-inch lengths

1 quart lamb or beef stock (see larder)

2 cups red wine

1½ cups cornmeal or polenta

2 cups whole milk

4 bay leaves

½ cup heavy cream

12 parsley roots, trimmed and halved lengthwise, plus 2 cups chopped fresh flat-leaf parsley leaves

1 tablespoon julienned lemon zest

2 tablespoons basic vinaigrette (see larder)

Preheat the oven to 190°F.

Season the lamb shanks with salt. In a heavy-bottomed braising pan over high heat, cook the lamb shanks in 2 tablespoons of the oil until browned, about 10 minutes. Add the onion, garlic and celery and cook until the celery is translucent, about 5 minutes more. Pour in the stock and wine and cook until simmering, then remove from the heat and place the pan in the oven. Bake until the lamb is very tender, about 4 hours. Transfer the lamb to a warm place.

In a medium pot over medium heat, whisk together the cornmeal, 5 cups cold water, milk, bay leaves and cream. Cook, stirring often, until the cornmeal is fully hydrated and thickened, about 30 minutes. Season with salt.

Increase the oven temperature to 500°F. In a small bowl, toss together the parsley roots, the remaining 1 tablespoon oil and salt to taste. Spread in a single layer on a baking sheet and bake until tender, 5 to 7 minutes. Transfer to a medium bowl and toss together with the parsley leaves, lemon zest and vinaigrette. Season with salt.

Divide the polenta among four warmed bowls. Top with lamb and a little broth. Finish each serving with some parsley salad.

"BRIAR RABBIT"

This dish was inspired by our farmstead, Bramble Hill, as we first found it, forlorn after decades of neglect. The gardens were overrun with thickets of wild roses, raspberries and brambleberries everywhere. And our share of rabbits, too. It is fitting that this dish is so good, as rabbit and brambleberries have an affinity for each other that goes well beyond a certain children's story. The smoky grilled potatoes add an earthiness that keeps the dish grounded and savory.

SERVES 4

1 cup raspberries
1 cup fresh wild roses
1 cup champagne vinegar
4 rabbit legs
2 tablespoons unsalted butter, softened
1 large onion, minced
2 tablespoons garlic, minced
1 quart rabbit stock (see tip, page 130), plus more if needed
2 cups white wine
12 baby carrots
¼ cup brandy
2 cups chicken stock (see larder)
2 cups red wine
2 tablespoons black peppercorns
12 fingerling potatoes
sea salt
sunflower oil
1 cup mixed raspberries and blackberries

In a glass jar, combine the raspberries, half of the wild roses and the vinegar, stirring well. Let sit for 1 hour, then strain the mixture through a fine sieve, pushing on the solids to extract as much liquid as possible. Set aside.

In a heavy-bottomed braising pan over high heat, combine the rabbit, butter, onion and garlic and cook until the onions begin to color, about 5 minutes. Add the stock and wine and reduce the heat to a simmer, cooking the rabbit until tender, about 2 hours. Add more stock or water if necessary to ensure the rabbit is always covered with liquid.

Add the baby carrots and cook until tender. Transfer the rabbit and carrots to a mixing bowl, add the reserved raspberry vinegar and let marinate for 1 hour.

Meanwhile, make the rose and raspberry jus: In a medium pot over high heat, combine the remaining ½ cup wild roses and the brandy. Bring to a boil, then reduce to a simmer. When reduced by three-quarters, add the stock, red wine and peppercorns. Simmer until the sauce is reduced by half, then strain and discard the solids from the sauce; keep warm.

In a medium pot over high heat, boil the potatoes in salted water until just tender, about 20 minutes. Strain the potatoes and place in a large bowl.

Add the rabbit and carrots to the large bowl of potatoes. Dress with oil and season with salt, if necessary, tossing gently. Grill the rabbit and potato mixture over charcoal or wood until lightly charred, or cook in a broiler until lightly browned, about 5 minutes.

Divide the rabbit and root vegetables among four warmed plates. Top each with some rose and raspberry jus and garnish with some raspberries and blackberries. Serve immediately.

GRILLED LAMB
WITH FATTOUSH & CUCUMBER YOGURT

Lamb dishes can easily become too heavy to serve during the summer. Here, I've paired sirloin of lamb with several substantial yet light sides that yield a perfect dish for the warm months. Fattoush is a salad of grilled fresh pita, tomatoes, herbs and feta cheese akin to the Tuscan panzanella salad but with a Middle Eastern feel. The cucumber yogurt adds a cooling freshness to it all.

SERVES 4

3 fresh pita breads
1 tablespoon olive oil
sea salt
2 cups sliced heirloom
    tomatoes
½ fennel bulb, shaved
1 cup crumbled feta cheese
1 small red onion, julienned
1½ cups chopped fresh cilantro
½ cup chopped fresh mint plus
    2 tablespoons minced
½ cup chopped fresh basil
½ cup diced pitted kalamata
    olives
1 cucumber, seeded and
    grated
2 cups plain yogurt
2 tablespoons minced fresh
    parsley
freshly ground black pepper
2 tablespoons extra-virgin
    olive oil
2 pounds lamb sirloin,
    trimmed

Brush the pita breads with the olive oil and season with salt. Grill over a charcoal or wood fire until lightly charred, about 1 minute on each side, or toast under the broiler. Tear into bite-sized pieces and transfer to a large bowl. Toss the grilled pita with the tomatoes, fennel, feta, onion, cilantro, the ½ cup chopped mint, basil and olives. Season with salt.

In a small bowl, toss together the cucumber, yogurt, the minced mint and parsley. Season with salt and pepper and stir in the extra-virgin olive oil.

Season the lamb with salt. Grill over a charcoal or wood fire until lightly charred and cooked to desired doneness, about 5 minutes on each side. Season with pepper. Transfer the lamb to a platter to rest for 5 to 10 minutes, then slice very thinly.

Divide the lamb among four plates. Top each with fattoush and cucumber yogurt. Serve immediately.

GRILLED LAMB CHOPS
WITH GREMOLATA & GRILLED SUMMER VEGETABLES

Quick to pick up a smoky char, grilled lamb chops are a favorite at our summer farm dinners, as they strike a balance between elegant and casual. I serve them here with height-of-the-season grilled vegetables and lots of garlic. Gremolata is a mixture of herbs, lemon zest and garlic, which, while simple, lifts the lamb's flavor with its vivid freshness.

SERVES 4

2 tablespoons minced garlic

2 tablespoons minced lemon zest

¼ cup minced fresh parsley

2 tablespoons minced fresh basil

2 tablespoons extra-virgin olive oil

2 zucchini or summer squash, cut into ¼-inch-thick slices

1 red pepper, cored and halved

1 eggplant, peeled and cut into ¼-inch-thick slices

2 cups Romano beans, picked

1 red onion, cut into ¼-inch-thick slices

3 tablespoons sunflower oil

sea salt

2 racks of lamb, trimmed, about 3 pounds total

freshly ground black pepper

In a small bowl, toss together the garlic, lemon zest, parsley, basil and olive oil. Set the gremolata aside.

In a large bowl, combine the zucchini, pepper, eggplant, beans, onion and sunflower oil, season with salt and toss well. Over a charcoal or wood fire, grill the vegetables until lightly charred, 4 to 5 minutes. Transfer to a serving platter.

Season the racks of lamb on both sides with salt and pepper. Grill the racks over the same fire, turning frequently, until cooked to an internal temperature of 129°F, as measured on a meat thermometer. Transfer to a platter and, while still very hot, generously dress the lamb with the gremolata. Let rest for 5 minutes.

Slice the lamb into chops at every other bone along the rack. Divide among four warmed plates. Garnish with the grilled vegetables and serve immediately.

SUMMER BEANS

I love fresh summer beans and we grow many types at the farm. Summer beans fall into three categories: filet beans, like the classic green bean or haricots verts; fresh shell beans, the tender version of what will eventually become winter-stored dried beans like pinto or black beans; and Romano beans, which produce a large edible pod like a standard green bean only much bigger. Sweet and crisp, they have a meaty quality due to their size. Romano beans excel on the grill as they are large enough to keep their toothsome texture.

RABBIT LOINS WITH HAM & PUMPKIN DUMPLINGS

When buying rabbit, I reserve the loins for this recipe, as they cook quickly and pair well with our dried ham. We cure our own hams in the restaurant, and often have 40 or more drying at a time. It is important to shave the ham very thinly when using as a wrapping for rabbit loins. Thin ham yields a toothsome but tender bite to the loins and an astounding depth of flavor.

SERVES 4

1 pound winter squash or
   pumpkin, peeled and diced
2 tablespoons sunflower oil
sea salt
1 cup semolina flour
2 cups chicken stock
   (see larder)
3 egg yolks
pinch of freshly grated nutmeg
1 cup all-purpose flour
5 tablespoons unsalted butter,
   softened
4 rabbit loins
freshly ground black pepper
6 paper-thin slices of country
   ham or prosciutto
2 sprigs fresh rosemary,
   cut into 1½-inch lengths
1 cup Brussels sprouts,
   separated into leaves
lemon juice to taste

Preheat the oven to 500°F.

In a medium bowl, toss together the squash, oil and salt to taste. Spread in a single layer on a baking sheet and roast in the oven until tender and beginning to brown, about 10 minutes. While still hot, transfer to the bowl of a food processor and purée until smooth, about 1 minute.

In a medium pot over high heat, whisk together the semolina, stock, 1 cup water and 1 teaspoon salt. Cook, stirring constantly, until the semolina has fully hydrated and is very thick, about 15 minutes. It will take on a glassy sheen when ready. Remove from the heat and stir in the squash purée. Return to the heat and cook until just warm. Stir in the egg yolks and season with salt and nutmeg.

Dusting your work surface with the all-purpose flour, roll the dough into finger-thick logs. Cut each into thumbnail-sized pieces. Boil the dumplings in batches without crowding in salted water until firm, about 5 minutes for each batch. Using a hand strainer, transfer the dumplings to a colander. In a large skillet over high heat, sauté the dumplings on one side in 2 tablespoons of butter until browned, about 5 minutes. Remove from the heat and set aside.

Season the rabbit loins lightly with salt and pepper. Wrap each loin in the ham and secure in place with rosemary sprigs.

In a large skillet over high heat, sauté the rabbit in 2 tablespoons of the butter until the ham is lightly crisped, about 2 minutes on each side. Transfer to a platter to rest. Return the pan to the stove and reduce the heat to medium. Add the remaining tablespoon of butter and the Brussels sprouts and cook until wilted, about 2 minutes. Season with salt and lemon juice.

Divide the rabbit loins among 4 warmed plates. Garnish with the dumplings and Brussels sprouts.

ROASTED LEG OF LAMB
WITH BORLOTTI BEANS

Roasting a whole leg of lamb makes for a memorable dinner. Few main dishes look as beautiful on a platter as this. I love to tuck lots of herbs and garlic into the pocket of the lamb, which yields a wonderful flavor inside and out. Winter savory, the perennial cousin of thyme, has a spicy, herbaceous note that lifts the flavor of the borlotti beans. Easy to grow, it is a smart addition to any kitchen herb garden. If it is unavailable, sprigs of thyme make a good substitution.

SERVES 4

2 tablespoons minced garlic

2 tablespoons minced lemon zest

¼ cup minced fresh parsley

2 tablespoons minced fresh sage

4 tablespoons olive oil

1 whole leg of lamb, about 5 pounds

salt and freshly ground black pepper

2 large leeks, green tops removed, diced

1 carrot, diced

1 tablespoon sunflower oil

2 cups fresh borlotti beans

2 cups chicken stock (see larder)

2 sprigs fresh winter savory

1 medium head escarole, outer leaves discarded and chopped

2 tablespoons freshly grated horseradish

Preheat the oven to 500°F.

In a small bowl, toss together the garlic, lemon zest, parsley, sage and 2 tablespoons of the olive oil. Season the lamb with salt and pepper, then rub the garlic mixture throughout the inside of the lamb leg. Tie the leg into a cylinder using butcher's twine.

Roast the lamb in the oven until it begins to brown, about 20 minutes. Lower the temperature to 300°F and cook until the internal temperature reads 129°F on a meat thermometer, about 45 minutes more.

Meanwhile, in a medium pot over medium-high heat, cook the diced leeks and carrot in the sunflower oil until the leeks are softened, about 7 minutes. Add the beans, stock and savory and cook until the beans are tender, about 10 minutes. Remove from the heat, add the remaining 2 tablespoons olive oil and season with salt. Set aside and keep warm.

Remove the lamb from the oven and let rest for 10 minutes, then transfer to a carving board and slice into very thin slices.

Return the roasting pan to the stovetop over medium heat. Add the escarole and cook until wilted, about 3 minutes. Season with salt.

Divide the lamb among four plates and add the leek and bean mixture alongside. Garnish with the escarole and horseradish and serve immediately.

Overleaf: Lamb confit crepinettes, in process and cooked (page 144)

STUFFED SADDLE OF LAMB
WITH BARLEY RISOTTO & CABBAGE

While a whole roasted saddle of lamb is a bit of extra work, the results are magic to behold. Perhaps the ultimate of dishes for entertaining, it marvels all who have the opportunity to enjoy it. Slow-cooked red wine cabbage is both an elegant and comforting accompaniment, to which I've added black cumin seeds for a touch of exotic perfume.

SERVES 6

1 pound ground lamb

4 ounces lamb fat, pork belly, or fatback, cut into small dice (available from your butcher)

1½ cups minced onion

3 tablespoons plus ¼ cup minced garlic, plus 3 tablespoons sliced

¼ cup barley wine ale

2 tablespoons caraway seeds

1 tablespoon whole-grain mustard

1 egg yolk

2 tablespoons plus ¼ cup heavy cream

1 whole lamb saddle, deboned

salt and freshly ground black pepper

2 slices bacon, diced

2 pounds red cabbage, thinly sliced

2 large red onions, sliced

2 cups red wine

¼ cup red wine vinegar

4 bay leaves

1 tablespoon black cumin seeds

1½ cups barley, toasted

2 tablespoon sunflower oil

1½ quarts vegetable or chicken stock (see larder)

freshly grated nutmeg to taste

1 tablespoon verjus (see note)

Preheat the oven to 450°F. In a medium bowl, mix the ground lamb, fat, ½ cup minced onion, 3 tablespoons of minced garlic, the ale, half the caraway, the mustard, egg yolk and 2 tablespoons cream.

Season the lamb saddle with salt and pepper. Stuff the loin cavity with the ground lamb mixture and roll to close. Tie with butcher's twine and place the stuffed loin in a heavy-bottomed roasting pan in the oven. Roast until the internal temperature measures 135°F on a meat thermometer, about 1½ hours. Remove from the oven and let rest for 10 minutes.

Meanwhile, in a large pot over medium-high heat, cook the bacon until just crisp, about 3 minutes. Add the cabbage, sliced red onions and garlic and cook until the onions are translucent, about 20 minutes. Add the wine, vinegar, 2 of the bay leaves, remaining 1 tablespoon caraway seeds and the cumin seeds and cook until the liquid has evaporated. Season with salt and pepper and keep warm.

In a medium pot over medium-high heat, cook the barley, the remaining 1 cup minced onion and ¼ cup minced garlic in the oil until the onion just begins to color, about 5 minutes. Add the stock and remaining 2 bay leaves and cook until the barley is tender, adding a little water if necessary. Pour in the remaining ¼ cup cream and season with salt, grated nutmeg, and the verjus.

Slice the lamb thinly and divide among six plates. Garnish each with the braised cabbage and barley risotto. Serve immediately.

- -

A TOUCH OF ACID

Most dishes benefit from a touch of acid at the end of cooking. Lemon or lime juice has a clean, transparent flavor and is my choice for simple dishes like sautéed asparagus. Yet there are complex acids, too, like vinegar, wine and verjus. Verjus is a vinegar-like liquid made from unripe, sour green grapes. Historically, winemakers prune their vines of excess grapes to concentrate the flavor in the bunches that remain. The pruned grapes find a use as a vinegar or wine substitute in cooking. The flavor of verjus is very sour and layered with vegetal, fruity notes. I love its savory quality for long, slow-cooked dishes.

LAMB CONFIT CREPINETTES

We raise the heritage breed of sheep called Tunis, which is very tender and deeply flavored with extensive marbling. The lamb's subtle perfume pairs well with aromatic spices and the crunch of cocoa nibs.

SERVES 4

- 2 pounds boneless lamb shoulder
- sea salt
- 1 quart pork or duck fat
- 2 cinnamon sticks
- 4 pieces star anise
- 8 cardamom pods
- 1 orange, halved
- 1 tablespoon smoked paprika
- freshly ground black pepper
- 2 cups caul fat (page 13)
- 3 cups lamb or beef stock (see larder)
- 2 cups red wine
- 1 whole clove
- 1 teaspoon whole grains of paradise
- 2 tablespoons cocoa nibs
- 1 tablespoon black currants
- 4 red peppers, sliced

Preheat the oven to 190°F. Season the lamb with salt. Place in a braising pot over medium heat, add the fat, 1 cinnamon stick, the star anise, 4 cardamom pods and the orange. Cook until the fat begins to simmer, about 6 minutes. Transfer to the oven and bake until the lamb is very tender, about 5 hours.

Remove the lamb from the fat and shred the meat. Mix in the paprika and check for seasoning. Cut the caul fat into four 7-inch circles and spread on a work surface. Top each with one quarter of the lamb and form into bundles, securing with toothpicks.

In a medium pot over high heat, combine the stock, wine, remaining stick of cinnamon, cardamom pods, the clove and grains of paradise. Bring to a boil, then simmer until reduced by half, about 40 minutes. Strain back into the pot to discard the spices, then add the cocoa and currants. Season with salt and keep warm.

Preheat the oven to 450°F. Place the red peppers on a baking sheet and top with the lamb. Bake until browned and cooked through, about 15 minutes.

Divide the lamb and peppers among four plates. Top with the spiced jus, cocoa and currants and serve.

LAMB TAGINE
WITH BLACK CHICKPEAS

This dish receives its name from the distinct vessel it is cooked and served in. Tagines are thrifty, comforting and delicious. In the restaurant, we use this as the focal point of a meal that often includes a fun collection of side dishes such as olives, preserved lemons, cooked greens, yogurt and couscous.

SERVES 4

- 2 cups dried black chickpeas
- sea salt
- 2 pounds lamb stew meat, diced
- 2 tablespoons sunflower oil
- 2 medium onions, diced
- 6 cloves garlic, sliced
- 12 baby carrots, trimmed
- 6 baby turnips, halved
- 12 baby potatoes
- 12 parsley roots
- 2 cinnamon sticks
- 2 tablespoons smoked paprika
- 1 tablespoon coriander seeds
- 1 tablespoon fennel seeds
- 1 tablespoon cumin seeds
- 1 teaspoon caraway seeds
- 1 dried lemon (see larder)
- 2 quarts lamb or beef stock (see larder)
- 1 cup Cerignola olives, pitted
- 1 tablespoon lemon zest
- ½ cup chopped fresh cilantro
- ¼ cup chopped fresh parsley

In a medium pot, mix the chickpeas with 1 quart water and soak overnight. Drain the water and replace with another quart of water seasoned with salt. Place over high heat and boil the chickpeas until tender, about 1½ hours. Drain through a colander and set aside.

In a large braising pot over high heat, combine the lamb and oil. Season with salt and cook until browned on all sides, about 15 minutes. Add the onions, garlic, root vegetables, spices and lemon and cook until very aromatic. Pour in the stock and reduce the heat to a simmer. Cook until the lamb is tender, about 2 hours.

Stir in the chickpeas and olives and simmer for 5 minutes. Divide the tagine among four large bowls. Top each with the lemon zest and herbs and serve.

"A REUNION" OF POACHED RABBIT
WITH FOIE GRAS & ROOT CONFIT

This is a serious dish, apart from the funny name. During the growing season, the wild rabbits around the farm are our constant companions, often hiding underfoot. In reality, wild rabbits don't make it into the kitchen despite the occasional threat we voice in their direction. The restaurant's rabbits are produced at the farm next door, Spring Tree Rabbitry, and you can find rabbit meat at your local butcher or farmer's market. Admittedly, adding truffles and foie gras to a dish like this is like gilding a lily. But sometimes gold leaf on flowers is gorgeous. Either way, it is a swoon-worthy dish.

SERVES 4

2 cups Sauternes wine
lemon juice
sea salt
4 sheets gelatin
½ cup diced orange carrots
½ cup diced yellow carrots
¼ cup diced parsnips
1 cup diced leeks
1 cup peeled and diced potato
½ cup peeled and diced salsify
   (see note, page 183)
6 cloves garlic
1½ quarts roasted garlic oil
   (see larder)
1 sprig fresh rosemary
8 rabbit loins
2 cups baby arugula leaves
1 tablespoons basic vinaigrette
   (see larder)
¼ cup shaved salt-cured foie
   gras (see larder)
2 tablespoons shaved black
   truffles

In a small pot over high heat, warm the wine at 180°F for 6 minutes to cook out the alcohol. Season with lemon juice and a touch of salt. Remove from the heat and let cool to just warm. Stir in the gelatin until fully dissolved. Line a small loaf pan with plastic wrap. Pour the wine into the pan and refrigerate until fully set and cool, about 2 hours. Chop the gelée into medium dice and keep chilled.

In a large pot over high heat, combine the root vegetables with enough water to cover. Season generously with salt; the water should taste of the sea. Bring to a boil then immediately strain through a colander. Return the root vegetables to the pot and combine with the garlic, garlic oil and rosemary. Return the pot to the stove and reduce the heat to a slight simmer. When the roots are tender, after about 30 minutes, remove with a hand strainer and set aside.

Season the rabbit loins with salt. Add to the hot oil in the pot and increase the oil temperature to 170°F. Cook the rabbit until it reaches an internal temperature of 140°F, as measured by a meat thermometer.

Dress the arugula with the vinaigrette and season with salt. Divide among four plates and top each with the winter roots and rabbit loin. Garnish each with foie gras, sliced truffles and the gelée.

HEIRLOOM CARROTS
For me, carrot varieties fall into two camps—some are best eaten raw while others shine when cooked. At the farm, we plant both types. For this dish, I naturally go for the cooking varieties: the yellow Jaune du Doubs, the orange Chantenay and Rothschild, and the bright red Atomic Red. Not grown to win beauty contests, they boast deep flavor that builds through long cooking.

WINTER HARVEST

Under a blanket of snow, much of the farm rests through the cold winter. The work pace slows and allows time to consider the successes and failures of the year as it comes to a close. While the harvests of oh-so-sweet winter field greens continue and the restaurants draw on the bounty stored in the root cellars, our attention shifts toward the next project: charcuterie. There is a great wisdom found in the old ways. Like it has been done for centuries, winter is the time to cull down the herd and, in turn, to make cured meats. We honor that tradition at Black Cat Farm. Through the heart of winter, we hang hams to smoke and then dry, make traditional cured sausages and confits. Practicing this craft keeps us attuned to the rhythms of the land and provides variety and interest to the wintertime plate.

BEEF

FOR MY BIRTHDAY, I GOT NUMBER 25 AND NUMBER 26, OUR SHAGGY SCOTTISH HIGHLAND CATTLE. I'D BEEN INTERESTED IN RAISING CATTLE FOR BEEF IN THE RESTAURANT, BUT I KNEW NOTHING ABOUT IT. YOU SEE, I'M NO RANCHER, I'M A FARMER. I'M STILL NOT A COWBOY, THOUGH. I HAVE TO WAIT FOR THE NEXT BIRTHDAY. I'M HOPING FOR A HAT AND BOOTS.

BRESOLE WITH ASPARAGUS, LEEKS & MINT

Bresole is a traditional Italian dish that combines thin slices of tender beef rolled with handmade sausage. In this version, I have taken some liberties by including asparagus and baby leeks in the filling. The first tender mint of the year adds a delightful freshness.

SERVES 4

1 pound beef shoulder, finely chopped, or ground beef

½ pound pork belly, finely chopped

1 medium white onion, finely chopped

¼ cup minced garlic

1 teaspoon ground fennel

2 teaspoon ground nutmeg

sea salt and freshly ground black pepper

2 leeks, green tops removed

24 stalks asparagus, peeled and trimmed

1 pound beef top round, thinly sliced and pounded

2 tablespoons sunflower oil

2 cups chicken stock (see larder)

1 tablespoon lemon zest

2 tablespoons verjus

¼ cup olive oil

1 cup julienned fresh mint

In the bowl of an electric mixer, combine the beef, pork, onion, garlic, fennel, and nutmeg. Season with salt and pepper and mix on low speed until the mixture begins to get sticky, 2 to 3 minutes. Cook 1 tablespoon in a small sauté pan to check the seasoning and adjust if necessary. Set aside in the refrigerator.

In a large stockpot over high heat, blanch the leeks in boiling salted water until just tender, about 5 minutes. Transfer the leeks to a colander to drain.

Blanch the asparagus in the same salted water until its color brightens, about 45 seconds. Transfer to the colander and immediately cool under running water. Dry with a towel.

On a clean work surface, spread a 12-inch-long piece of plastic wrap crosswise. Working from the bottom edge, top the plastic with half of the sliced beef to form a 5 by 10-inch rectangle. Spread half of the sausage mixture on top of the beef in a thin layer. Top with half of the leeks and 4 stalks of asparagus and season with salt. Using the plastic wrap, tightly roll the beef into a log shape, making sure the plastic stays on the outside of the roll. Compress the roll to remove any trapped air and remove the plastic wrap altogether. Repeat the process using the remaining beef, sausage and vegetables, reserving 16 of the asparagus stalks for the next step.

In a large sauté pan over high heat, sauté the beef in the oil until lightly browned on all sides. Stir in the stock, zest and verjus, scraping up the browned bits from the pan and turning the beef occasionally. Cook until the rolls are browned but the interiors are still rosy, 10 to 12 minutes. Transfer the beef to a platter and whisk the olive oil into the pan. Season the sauce with salt. Add the remaining asparagus to the pan and warm through.

Slice each bresole into 6 pieces. Divide among four dinner plates and top with the sauce. Garnish with the asparagus and mint and serve immediately.

WONDRA FLOUR

For quick sautés when you want to crisp ingredients up, I recommend Wondra flour over regular all-purpose. Wondra is precooked, then dried and ground, resulting in added crispness and better flavor. With thinly sliced ingredients, like scallopini or the schnitzel below, often there is not enough time to cook the raw flour taste out of standard flour without turning the meat into shoe leather. The alternative is undercooking the flour, which leaves a pastiness. Wondra let's us have our cake and eat it too, or our schnitzel, as the case may be. While time-consuming to slice and pound out the meat, this is a surprisingly fast dish to sauté—less than 3 minutes.

SCHNITZEL WITH SORREL & BABY RADISHES

There are as many types of schnitzel as there are days in the year. I enjoy cooking schnitzel with the least amount of breading possible, which yields meat tender in the center and crispy on the edges. Here, I pair it with sorrel, a tart leafy herb that adds acidity to cut through the richness of the beef. A quick sauté of baby radishes in the pan drippings add a zesty crunch.

SERVES 4

2 pounds beef top round, thinly sliced against the grain and pounded (see tip, page 159)

sea salt

2 cups Wondra flour (see note, above)

¼ cup sunflower oil

3 cups baby radishes, trimmed

2 tablespoons minced lemon zest

¼ cup unsalted butter, softened

1 cup julienned sorrel

1 lemon, cut into wedges

Season the beef with salt. Dredge the beef slices in the flour on only one side, shaking off the excess. In a large sauté pan over high heat, sauté the beef in the oil, a few slices at a time, until they begin to brown, about 2 minutes. Turn the beef slices over and cook for 30 seconds more. Transfer the beef to a platter and continue sautéing until all of the beef is used up.

Add the radishes to the pan. Sauté until the radishes are warmed through, about 2 minutes. Remove the pan from the heat. Stir in the lemon zest and butter until the butter has melted. Add the sorrel and toss.

Divide the beef among four dinner plates. Top with the buttered radishes and sorrel. Squeeze a little fresh lemon juice over each serving and serve immediately.

BEEF POT AU FEU: POACHED BEEF, CAULIFLOWER & WATERCRESS IN A GINGER-SHRIMP BROTH

Taking cues from Chinese cuisine, I've combined meat and seafood to create a broth that resonates with deep flavor. The cauliflower adds a tender crunch and the watercress adds a spice note similar to wasabi. I look for richly marbled cuts of beef such as short ribs, shanks, chuck and neck for this dish, as they yield a velvety smooth texture after cooking.

SERVES 4

2 cups cauliflower florets
2 pounds beef chuck, or
   3 pounds bone-in neck
1 tablespoon sunflower oil
1 medium onion, diced
2 tablespoons sliced ginger
¼ cup minced garlic
2 quarts beef stock
   (see larder)
one 5-inch piece dried
   kombu seaweed
1 stalk lemongrass, chopped
2 tablespoons dried shrimp
sea salt
12 baby onions, trimmed
12 baby carrots, trimmed
4 spring onions, cut into
   2-inch lengths
2 tablespoons rice vinegar
½ cup watercress leaves
1 tablespoon sesame oil

In a medium pot over high heat, blanch the cauliflower in boiling salted water until tender. Refresh under running water or ice. Set aside.

In a heavy-bottomed braising pan over high heat, cook the beef in the oil until browned, about 10 minutes. Toss in the onion, ginger and garlic and cook for 4 minutes more. Add the stock, seaweed, lemongrass and dried shrimp. Season the broth with salt. Reduce the heat to low and cover the pot. Simmer until the beef is very tender, about 6 hours. After browning, a slow cooker may also be used to cook the beef.

Transfer the beef to a platter and using a fine sieve, strain the broth into a clean, large pot. Return the pot to low heat and add the baby onions, carrots and beef. Poach until the vegetables are just tender. Add the cauliflower and the spring onions. Season the broth with salt and add the rice vinegar.

In a small bowl, dress the watercress with the sesame oil. Season with salt and toss.

Divide the beef and vegetables among four large bowls. Top each with the hot broth and watercress and serve immediately.

BEEF BRISKET WITH BLUE CHEESE FRITTERS, MARINATED TOMATOES & GRILLED ONIONS

While braising beef normally evokes thoughts of cold winter nights, here I have created a dish that shows the technique is also a good fit for warm sultry nights. The blue cheese fritters and grilled onions add a fun, festive note while the chilled marinated tomatoes lend the dish a light summery air. Often I'll braise the beef a day ahead and then warm it outside on the grill just prior to dinner, which keeps the kitchen cooler on hot nights.

SERVES 4

2 pounds beef brisket

sea salt

2 tablespoons sunflower oil, plus more for frying

1 large onion, diced, plus 1 large Spanish onion, peeled and cut into ¼-inch-thick slices

¼ cup minced garlic

1½ quarts beef stock (see larder)

1 sprig fresh rosemary

2 cups heirloom tomatoes, cut into thick slices

5 tablespoons olive oil

1 tablespoon red wine vinegar

4 sprigs fresh thyme

1½ cups rice flour

¾ cup crumbled Maytag blue cheese

2 tablespoons chopped fresh parsley, plus ¼ cup parsley leaves

¾ cup wheat or light beer

Preheat the oven to 200°F.

Season the beef with salt. In an ovenproof braising pan over medium heat, sauté the beef in 1 tablespoon of the sunflower oil until browned, about 10 minutes. Add the diced onion and garlic and cook until the onion begins to brown, about 4 minutes. Add the stock and rosemary and place the beef, covered, in the oven to braise until the meat is very tender, about 6 hours. Remove the meat from the oven and keep warm. After browning, the beef could be alternatively cooked in a slow cooker.

In a medium bowl, toss the sliced onion with the remaining 1 tablespoon sunflower oil until evenly coated. Season with salt. Grill the onions over a wood or charcoal fire until lightly charred, about 3 minutes per side. Mince ¼ cup of the grilled onions and set aside. Return the rest of the grilled onions to the bowl and toss with the tomatoes, 3 tablespoons of the olive oil, the vinegar and thyme. Season with salt and set aside.

Heat 2 inches of sunflower oil in a large sauté pan until it shimmers.

Meanwhile, in a medium bowl, combine the rice flour, cheese, chopped parsley and reserved ¼ cup minced grilled onion. Season with salt then pour in the beer. Stir gently to combine. The batter should be as thick as mashed potatoes. Using a tablespoon, drop spoonfuls into the hot oil to fry until golden on both sides. Using a slotted spoon, transfer the fritters to paper towels to drain and season with salt if necessary. Continue until all the batter is used up.

Cut the beef into thick slices and divide among four warmed plates. Add the fritters and tomato and onions. Drizzle with the remaining 2 tablespoons olive oil and sprinkle with the parsley leaves. Serve immediately.

GRILLED RIB-EYE
WITH CHILLED BRAISED CELERY

Grilled rib-eye served in the summer does not need much adornment. The braised celery fondant adds a rich background flavor and strong herbaceousness while the freshly grated horseradish adds zest and spice. Crisp fried capers add bursts of salty crunch.

SERVES 4

3 cups celery, peeled and cut into 1-inch pieces	2 tablespoons capers, patted dry
2 tablespoons minced garlic	2 tablespoons sunflower oil
2 tablespoons unsalted butter, softened	4 beef rib-eye steaks, about 8 ounces each
2 cups chicken stock	freshly ground black pepper
2 tablespoons lovage leaves	2 tablespoons extra-virgin olive oil
½ cup crème fraîche	2 tablespoons freshly grated horseradish
sea salt	
apple cider vinegar	

In a medium saucepan over medium heat, cook the celery and garlic in the butter until translucent, about 6 minutes. Add the stock and simmer until reduced by three-quarters, about 1 hour. Reserve 6 pieces of the celery and transfer the remaining celery with the lovage leaves to a blender. Purée until very smooth, about 5 minutes. Add the crème fraîche and purée for 1 minute. Chill until cold, at least 2 hours. Season with salt and vinegar and set aside.

In a small sauté pan over medium-high heat, sauté the capers in the sunflower oil until crisp, about 4 minutes. Drain on paper towels.

Season the steaks with salt. Grill over a wood or charcoal fire until lightly charred. Transfer to a platter, season with pepper and drizzle with the olive oil.

Divide the steaks among four warmed plates. Garnish with the reserved celery and the chilled purée. Top with the capers and horseradish and serve.

PEPPERY GRILLED BEEF
WITH YOGURT & HARICOTS VERTS

Combining grilled meats with fresh peppery spices often leads to spectacular results. In addition to seasoning the beef with the standard pepper, I've added grains of paradise and cardamom to the mix to add a spicy floral note. The spiced yogurt has a cooling effect that balances the heat of the beef. Fresh haricots verts, served simply, bring a sweetness to the dish.

SERVES 4

¼ cup minced onion	2 cups plain yogurt
2 teaspoons ground coriander	1 cup grated cucumber
1 teaspoon ground cardamom, plus 1 pod, ground	sea salt
	3 cups haricots verts, trimmed
1 teaspoon ground fennel	2 tablespoons olive oil
freshly ground black pepper	1 tablespoon lemon zest
	1½ cups shallot confit (see larder)
2 teaspoons ground grains of paradise	4 beef rib-eye steaks, about 6 ounces each

In a medium bowl, combine the onion, coriander, 1 teaspoon cardamom, the fennel, 1 teaspoon pepper, 1 teaspoon of the grains of paradise, the yogurt and cucumber. Season with salt, mix well and set aside.

Steam the haricots verts in a steamer basket set over boiling water for about 3 minutes. Transfer to a bowl and toss with the oil, lemon zest and shallot confit. Season with salt and pepper and keep warm.

Season the steaks with salt. Over a wood or charcoal fire, grill the steaks until lightly charred. Transfer to a platter and season with pepper, the remaining cardamom and grains of paradise.

Divide the steaks among four warmed plates. Top each with the haricots verts and yogurt sauce.

SCALOPPINI WITH GOLDEN TURNIPS & RAPINI

Scaloppini is simply a quick sauté of thinly sliced beef. After sautéing, the browned bits in the pan become the base for a flavorful mustard sauce. Rapini, broccoli's more assertive brother, adds a pleasant bitterness that cleanses the palate. The olives add an occasional burst of salt and paradoxically balance the rapini's bitter edge.

SERVES 4

2 cups gold turnips, peeled and cut into wedges

sea salt

2 tablespoons plus ¼ cup sunflower oil

1 cup chicken stock (see larder)

2 bay leaves

freshly ground black pepper

2 tablespoons unsalted butter

2 teaspoons minced garlic

3 cups chopped rapini

2 pounds beef top round or sirloin, thinly sliced against the grain and pounded (see tip)

½ cup flour, preferably Wondra (see note, page 151)

3 tablespoons white wine

1 cup beef stock (see larder)

1 tablespoon Dijon mustard

¼ cup olive oil

½ cup pitted olives

In a medium pot over high heat, blanch the turnips in boiling salted water until tender. Strain through a colander and place the turnips in a medium stainless-steel sauté pan over high heat. Add 1 tablespoon of the sunflower oil and sauté the turnips until browned. Reduce the heat to medium and pour in the chicken stock, bay leaves and a grind of black pepper. Cook until the stock has reduced almost fully. Add the butter and season with salt, stirring well, until the butter has melted and glazed the turnips. Keep warm.

In a medium sauté pan over high heat, sauté the garlic in 1 tablespoon of the sunflower oil until it just begins to color, about 30 seconds. Add the rapini and a little splash of water and cook until wilted and heated through. Season with salt and keep warm.

Season the beef with salt. Place the flour in a shallow bowl and dredge the beef on one side with the flour, shaking off the excess. In batches, sauté the beef in the remaining ¼ cup sunflower oil until lightly browned, 2 to 3 minutes. Turn the pieces over and cook for 15 seconds more. Transfer to a platter and repeat until all of the beef is used up.

Add the wine and beef stock to the pan. Scrape the browned bits from the pan to loosen them. Reduce the heat to medium and cook until the sauce thickens slightly. Whisk in the mustard and olive oil.

Divide the beef among four dinner plates. Garnish with the turnips, rapini and olives. Top the beef with the sauce and serve immediately.

COOKING TIP

Top round and sirloin are the cuts I prefer for making both scaloppini and schnitzel, as these cuts are tender and free of excess connective tissue. Preparing the meat is a two-step process: thinly slicing followed by pounding. Take extra care to slice the meat about ⅛-inch thick, which makes the pounding go very quickly and yields perfectly tender cutlets every time. I've made the mistaken "shortcut" of slicing thicker pieces of beef and then pounding until my arm fell off. The result was as chewy as rawhide.

CORNED BEEF TONGUE
WITH PARSLEY ROOT & ROASTED SHALLOTS

I was introduced to corned beef tongue by my grandmother, who served it only one way: with parsnips and spicy mustard. Here, I have taken my grandmother's dish and varied it a bit: parley roots stand in for the parsnips, roasted shallots provide sweetness and fresh horseradish spice. The tongue will need to brine for two days before cooking.

SERVES 4

sea salt
1 tablespoon curing salt
¼ cup brown sugar
2 tablespoons celery seed
1 tablespoon black
    peppercorns
½ teaspoon ground clove
1 teaspoon ground nutmeg
5 bay leaves
2 pounds beef tongue
1 medium onion, quartered
1 carrot, chopped
1 rib of celery, chopped
1 pound parsley roots, peeled
    and trimmed
3 tablespoons sunflower oil
1 cup vegetable stock
4 tablespoons unsalted butter
lemon juice to taste
2 tablespoons chopped fresh
    parsley
1 cup peeled whole shallots
¼ cup red wine
freshly ground black pepper
freshly grated horseradish

In a medium pot over high heat, combine 1 cup water with 1 cup salt, the curing salt, brown sugar, spices and 4 bay leaves. Boil for 1 minute and remove from the heat. Cool the brine completely before combining the beef tongue and brine in a suitably sized container and refrigerating for 2 days.

Remove the tongue from the brine and rinse under cold water. Place in a pot and cover with water. Add the onion, carrot and celery and season lightly with salt. Set over high heat and boil for 1 minute, then reduce the heat to a bare simmer and cook until the tongue is tender, 4 to 5 hours.

In a medium sauté pan over high heat, sauté the parsley roots in 2 tablespoons of the sunflower oil until lightly browned, about 7 minutes. Add the stock or water, season with salt and cook until reduced. Reduce the heat to low and stir in half of the butter until melted. Season with lemon juice and add the parsley. Set aside.

In a small sauté pan over high heat, sauté the whole shallots in the remaining tablespoon sunflower oil until browned, about 7 minutes. Add the wine and remaining bay leaf, reduce the heat to medium and cook until the wine is fully reduced, about 10 minutes. Off the heat, add the remaining 2 tablespoons butter, season with salt and pepper and stir until the butter has melted.

Peel the skin off of the tongue with a sharp paring knife and thinly slice the tongue. Divide among four dinner plates and garnish with the parsley roots and shallots. Grate fresh horseradish over and serve immediately.

BRAISED BEEF SHORT RIBS
WITH GNOCCHI, CARDOONS & KALE

This is one of my favorite ways to serve slow-cooked short ribs. The gnocchi are a variation on the traditional recipe using fresh goat cheese in lieu of the potato. Properly called *gnudi*, they yield toothsome pasta with better flavor than the potato version. Cardoons, a cousin of artichokes, have a similar flavor and, like celery, are grown for their leaf ribs.

SERVES 4

2 pounds beef short ribs, cut into 4 equal pieces

1 tablespoon salt, plus more for seasoning

5 tablespoons sunflower oil

2 ribs celery, chopped

2 large carrots, sliced

1 large onion, peeled and quartered, plus 2 medium onions, diced

1 quart beef or chicken stock (see larder)

2 cups red wine

1 sprig fresh rosemary plus 1 tablespoon minced

2 sprigs fresh sage

2 cups bread flour

2 cups plus 2 tablespoons fresh goat cheese

2 large eggs

1 pound cardoons, peeled and cut into ½-inch-thick slices

¼ cup roasted garlic (see larder)

2 cups chicken or vegetable stock (see larder)

4 sprigs fresh oregano

½ cup heavy cream

2 teaspoons minced garlic

1 bunch kale, stems discarded, chopped

2 tablespoons olive oil

Preheat the oven to 200°F.

Season the beef with the salt. In an ovenproof braising pan over medium heat, sauté the beef in 2 tablespoons of the sunflower oil until browned, about 10 minutes. Add the celery, carrots and quartered onion and cook until the onion begins to brown, about 4 minutes. Add the beef stock and wine and transfer the pan, covered, to the oven to braise until the meat is very tender, about 6 hours. Add additional broth or water to the pan as necessary. Season with salt and add the rosemary sprig and sage during the last hour of cooking. Remove the meat from the oven and keep warm.

In a large stockpot over high heat, bring salted water to a boil.

Meanwhile, in the bowl of a stand mixer fitted with the paddle, combine the flour, 2 cups of cheese, the eggs, minced rosemary and a pinch of salt. Mix on low speed until the dough pulls away from the sides of the bowl, about 5 minutes. Transfer to a floured work surface and split into two equal parts. Using a little flour on the pin, roll the dough into a long log about ¾ inch in diameter. Cut crosswise into ¾-inch-long pieces. Continue until the dough is used up.

Boil the dough in the salted water until the gnocchi are firm, about 7 minutes. Drain in a colander and set aside.

In a medium pot over high heat, boil the cardoons in salted water until tender, about 25 minutes. Drain through a colander and return to the pot. Add the diced onions, roasted garlic and 2 tablespoons of the sunflower oil. Cook until the onions begin to brown, about 7 minutes. Add the stock and oregano, reduce the heat to a simmer and cook until the vegetables are very tender, about 20 minutes. Season with salt. Strain through a colander and discard the broth.

Transfer half of the cardoon mixture to the bowl of a blender and purée until very smooth. With the motor running, add the cream and 2 tablespoons goat cheese. Season with salt and set aside.

In a large sauté pan over high heat, sauté the minced garlic in the remaining 1 tablespoon sunflower oil until just beginning to brown. Add the remaining cardoon mixture and the kale and season with salt. Cook until the kale is wilted. Add the reserved gnocchi and olive oil.

Spread the purée on the bottom of four dinner plates. Add a short rib to each plate and garnish with the wilted kale and gnocchi. Serve immediately.

WINTER ON THE FARM

While the pace of the farm slows in winter there is always plenty to do. The farm operates year-round to supply the restaurants; in winter, it's a great challenge. There are animals to keep warm and happy, equipment and water lines to keep from freezing, not to mention our fingers and toes. Even moving from place to place is a workout in deep, snowy fields. Harvesting field greens for the restaurants is the biggest challenge. When buried under a thick layer of snow, we wield long push brooms to gently liberate the rows a few feet at a time. After sweeping off the snow, we peel back the protective covers above the harvest, exposing the sweet, delicious greens underneath. I'm amazed we can pull it off; a glorious harvest found below such a bleak wintry scene. But in the challenge lies the integrity and it's the integrity that lets us sleep soundly, warm in our beds.

CARDOONS

More than most vegetables I sell at the farmer's market, cardoons need a quick recipe to go along with the purchase. I have to admit, most of my recipes come from conversations with the Italian transplants that frequent our stand. Their reaction to seeing the crates of cardoons is nothing short of shouts of pure joy: "Cardoni! Cardoni!" All cardoon recipes share a common braising step. First, the ribs are peeled to remove the spines and tough outer fibers. I keep lemon halves handy to rub the exposed surfaces to prevent browning. Next, the ribs are cut into manageable lengths and braised in water or stock until tender. In Sicily, the braised cardoons are breaded lightly and fried crisp to contrast their buttery artichoke-like interiors, and accompanied by a simple lemony aïoli. Another swoon-worthy dish is a gratin with the braised ribs topped with mint and pine nuts. Unless you are cooking for a big Sicilian family, there will probably be leftover cardoons from the braising step. I store these in a glass container in the fridge, covered with a simple vinaigrette of lemon, olive oil and oregano, for months.

BLANQUETTE OF WINTER VEGETABLES
WITH BREAST OF BEEF

The classic French blanquette, a cold weather stew defined by rich, subtle flavors melded together in its luxurious white sauce, is both simple and refined. I combine it here with beef cooked gently in a sturdy red wine. It is a marvel. Chervil survives deep into winter and provides fresh vitality to this rich dish.

SERVES 4

2 pounds beef breast

sea salt

5 tablespoons plus
    2 teaspoons sunflower oil

1 medium onion, peeled
    and quartered, plus 2
    tablespoons minced onion

6 cloves garlic, peeled, plus
    1 tablespoon minced garlic

2 cups beef or veal stock
    (see larder)

3 cups red wine

5 bay leaves

4 sprigs fresh thyme

2 magenta turnips, trimmed
    and quartered

12 baby carrots, peeled and
    trimmed

16 pearl onions, peeled

2 parsnips, peeled and sliced

8 baby or fingerling potatoes

3 tablespoons unsalted butter

2 tablespoons all-purpose
    flour

1½ cups chicken stock
    (see larder)

½ cup white wine

1 cup heavy cream

freshly grated nutmeg

½ cup chervil, chopped

1 dash sherry vinegar

Preheat the oven to 190°F.

Season the beef with the salt. In an ovenproof braising pan over medium heat, sauté the beef in 1 tablespoon of the oil until browned, about 10 minutes. Add the onion, garlic and 2 teaspoons of the oil and cook until the onion begins to brown, about 4 minutes. Pour in the beef stock and red wine and bring to a boil. Cover and transfer to the oven and braise the meat until very tender, about 6 hours. Lightly season the broth and add 3 bay leaves and the thyme during the last hour of cooking. Meanwhile, in a small pot over high heat, blanch the turnips in boiling salted water until just tender, about 7 minutes. Drain through a colander.

In a heavy-bottomed roasting pan over medium heat, combine the carrots, pearl onions, parsnips and potatoes with the ¼ cup oil. Cook until just tender, about 15 minutes. Add the turnips and season with salt. Set aside off the heat.

In a medium saucepan over medium-high heat, combine the butter, minced onion, and minced garlic and cook until translucent, about 5 minutes. Add the flour and cook, stirring continuously, until it begins to color. Stir in the remaining 2 bay leaves, the chicken stock and white wine. Scrape down the pan to loosen any stuck bits of flour and cook until the sauce thickens, about 7 minutes. Add the cream and cook for 4 minutes more. Season with salt and nutmeg.

Pour the sauce over the cooked vegetables and return to the stovetop over low heat to keep warm. Thin with a little water or extra cream if necessary.

In a small bowl, combine the chervil, 2 teaspoons of oil and the vinegar. Season with salt and toss well.

When the beef has finished braising, transfer to a cutting board. Return the pan to the stove over high heat and boil until the broth is reduced by half. Cut the braised beef into 4 equal portions and return to the pan with the reduced stock and keep warm.

Divide the beef among four dinner plates. Garnish with the vegetable blanquette and the chervil. Drizzle the beef with the reduced stock and serve immediately.

BEEF RAVIOLI WITH RADICCHIO & TAPENADE

Handmade ravioli are a joy to eat. Here, I fill them with braised beef and ricotta. Winter tames radicchio's assertiveness, and its deep garnet color provides an antidote to the winter cold. I often pair it with a salty component, as salt helps to temper its bitterness. The tapenade and ricotta salata serve that end.

SERVES 4

2 cups radicchio leaves

sea salt

4 tablespoons olive oil

½ cup kalamata olives, pitted

2 teaspoons minced onion

1 teaspoon minced garlic

1 tablespoon fresh parsley
  leaves

lemon juice to taste

1 pound braised beef,
  finely chopped

1 cup ricotta cheese

2 tablespoons heavy cream

¼ cup roasted garlic
  (see larder)

1 tablespoon minced
  fresh sage

pasta dough (see larder)

½ cup sliced ricotta salata

In a small bowl, toss the radicchio with 1 tablespoon salt and marinate for 30 minutes. Rinse well to remove excess salt then twist the radicchio dry. Dress with 1 tablespoon of the olive oil and set aside.

In the bowl of a food processor, finely chop the olives, onion, garlic and parsley. Season with lemon juice, add 1 tablespoon olive oil and toss. Set aside.

In a medium bowl, combine the beef, ricotta, cream, roasted garlic and sage. Season with salt and mix well. In a small bowl, combine 1 egg with 2 tablespoons of water. Mix the egg wash well and set aside.

Working with one piece of pasta dough at a time, roll to a ¼-inch thickness. Using a pasta machine on setting 1, roll the dough until smooth. Change the setting to 2 and pass the dough through again. Continue until the dough has been rolled through setting 6. The sheet will be very long at this point.

Cut the sheet into two equal pieces. On a lightly floured work surface, lay out the sheets, one above the other. On one sheet, every 3 inches, place 1 tablespoon of beef filling. Brush the pasta with the egg wash. Lay the second sheet on top and gently form over the beef and onto the bottom sheet. Press firmly to adhere. Cut halfway between each tablespoon of filling to form raviolis. Lightly flour to prevent sticking. Repeat with the 3 remaining sheets of pasta until the filling is used up. Wrap leftover pasta in plastic and freeze.

In a large stockpot of boiling salted water, boil the raviolis until al dente, about 3 minutes. Using a hand strainer, transfer the raviolis to a large bowl and immediately drizzle with the remaining 2 tablespoons olive oil to prevent them from sticking. Add the salted radicchio and toss well.

Divide the raviolis and radicchio among four warmed dinner plates. Top with the tapenade and ricotta salata and serve immediately.

COOKING TIP

If "life" happens to get in the way of making a good braise and yours ends up a touch too dry, adding a few extra tablespoons of heavy cream or some soft butter to the filling will moisten the beef. Serving the ravioli with a quick cream sauce helps, too.

ROAST BEEF TENDERLOIN WITH PONDEROSA PINE

In thinking about how to use native plants in the kitchen I came across ponderosa pine, which smells like a cross between cinnamon and vanilla. Many red wines share these same notes so it seemed possible to create a red wine–focused dish using the scent of ponderosa. Parsnip and vanilla work well together and reinforce that vanilla perfume often found in new world red wine.

SERVES 4

¼ cup ponderosa pine bark

½ cup brandy

6 shallots, peeled and halved

2 tablespoons sunflower oil

1 cup red wine

2 cups beef or veal stock (see larder)

½ vanilla bean plus 1 vanilla bean, split and scraped

1 bay leaf

10 black peppercorns

¾ pound parsnips, peeled and chopped

5 cloves garlic, peeled

½ cup heavy cream

sea salt

2 pounds beef tenderloin, cut into 4-ounce portions

2 tablespoons rendered duck or pork fat

freshly ground black pepper

In a small saucepan over low heat, combine the pine bark and brandy and bring to a simmer, about 3 minutes. Remove the pot from the heat and cool overnight. Strain the infused brandy into a clean container.

In a medium saucepan over medium-high heat, cook the shallots in 1 tablespoon of the oil until browned, about 10 minutes. Add the infused brandy, wine, stock, the ½ vanilla bean, bay leaf, and peppercorns and boil for 1 minute, then reduce the heat to a simmer. Cook until reduced by half, about 1 hour. Strain through a fine sieve and return to the pan, discarding the solids. Keep warm.

In a medium stockpot over medium heat, combine the parsnips, garlic and the remaining 1 tablespoon oil. Cook until the garlic just begins to color, about 5 minutes. Add enough water to cover and increase the temperature to high. Add the scraped vanilla bean and boil until the liquid is reduced by three-quarters. Discard the vanilla bean and transfer the mixture to the bowl of a food processor. Purée until very smooth, about 4 minutes. With the motor running, add the cream and mix until incorporated. Season with salt.

Season the beef with salt. In a large sauté pan over high heat, melt the fat. When the pan and fat are very hot, sauté the beef, turning occasionally, until browned on both sides, about 1½ minutes per side for rare, 2 minutes per side for medium rare. Remove the beef from the pan and season with pepper.

Divide the beef among four dinner plates. Place a scoop of the parsnip purée next to the beef and top the beef with the sauce. Serve immediately.

FISH

SOURCING FRESH, DELICIOUS FISH COMES DOWN TO TURNOVER. THAT IS,

THE FISHMONGER WHO SELLS THE MOST FISH ALSO SELLS THE FRESHEST FISH.

MOST OF THE FISH IN THIS CHAPTER ARE AVAILABLE THROUGH YOUR LOCAL

FISHMONGER. YOURS CAN EASILY PLACE A SPECIAL ORDER FOR YOU.

SAUTÉED HALIBUT
WITH BLUE CRAB NOODLES

Halibut is a firm-textured fish that stands up to robust presentations. The udon noodles dressed in blue crab offer a delicious accompaniment to the fish. The idea came from playing with the Chinese restaurant standard, egg fu young.

SERVES 4

1 cup diced leeks	julienned fresh ginger
2 tablespoons minced garlic	sea salt
1 tablespoon plus 2 teaspoons sesame oil	2 tablespoons julienned pickled ginger (see larder)
4 tablespoons sunflower oil	2 teaspoons rice wine vinegar
½ cup fish stock (see larder)	pinch of sugar
1 large egg	1 cup totsoi leaves (see note, page 54)
½ pound blue crab, picked	1 cup pea tendrils or other baby greens
1 pound udon noodles	1½ pounds halibut, cut into 6-ounce portions
1 cup spring onions	

In a medium sauté pan over medium heat, combine the leeks, garlic and 1 tablespoon each of the sesame and sunflower oils with 1 tablespoon water. Cook until the leeks are softened and translucent, about 4 minutes. Add the stock, egg, crab, noodles, spring onions and ginger. Season with salt and mix well. Cook until the egg thickens, about 4 minutes. Keep warm.

In a medium bowl, whisk together the pickled ginger, 2 teaspoons each of sesame and sunflower oils, the vinegar and sugar. Add the totsoi and pea tendrils, season with salt and toss gently to coat the leaves.

Season the halibut with salt. In a large pan over high heat, sauté the fillets in the remaining sunflower oil until golden, about 5 minutes. Turn the fillets over and cook until flaky and golden, about 7 minutes.

Divide the noodles among four plates and top with the halibut. Garnish with the totsoi salad and serve.

RISOTTO WITH RAPINI,
SPECK & BAY SCALLOPS

The trick to successful seafood in risotto is to add it after it has finished cooking. The residual heat of the risotto is more than enough to cook the little bay scallops. The addition of speck, a type of cured, smoked pork from the shoulder, adds a rich depth to the dish. Rapini and pistachios keep the dish alive with variations in flavor and texture.

SERVES 4

1 large onion, finely diced	sea salt
¼ cup plus 1 tablespoon minced garlic	1½ cups bay scallops, rinsed
4 tablespoons sunflower oil	1 cup shaved speck
2 cups Arborio rice	4 cups chopped rapini
1½ quarts vegetable or pork stock (see larder)	2 teaspoons minced lemon zest
1 cup white wine	2 tablespoons olive oil
3 bay leaves	¼ cup chopped toasted pistachios

In a large saucepan over high heat, combine the onion, ¼ cup garlic and 3 tablespoons of the sunflower oil. Cook, stirring often, until the onion just begins to color, about 4 minutes. Stir in the rice and cook, stirring constantly, for a minute more. Add 2 cups of the stock, the wine and bay leaves and cook, stirring often, until the liquid is nearly absorbed. Repeat with the remaining stock until it is all used up. Season with salt, remove from the heat and fold in the scallops and speck. Divide the risotto among four dinner plates.

In a large sauté pan over high heat, sauté the remaining 1 tablespoon garlic in the remaining 1 tablespoon sunflower oil for 1 minute. Add the rapini and a splash of water and sauté until wilted, about 2 minutes. Toss in the lemon zest and season with salt.

Top the plated risotto with rapini. Drizzle with the olive oil and garnish with the pistachios. Serve immediately.

RED LENTIL-CRUSTED GROUPER WITH SAAG

Crusting fish or seafood in lentils is a fun and easy way to add complexity, crunch and delicious flavor. I discovered the technique while experimenting with making flours from different grains. This lentil crust not only adds texture but a layer of flavor, too. The curry spices seem a fitting accompaniment as does the bright citrus and saag, a traditional curried spinach.

SERVES 4

1 medium onion, diced

¼ cup minced garlic

1 tablespoon minced
   fresh ginger

2 tablespoons curry powder
   (see larder)

4 tablespoons plus ¼ cup
   sunflower oil

8 cups chopped spinach

¼ cup yogurt

sea salt

2 tablespoons chopped
   orange zest

2 tablespoons chopped
   lemon zest

1 tablespoons sugar

lemon juice

1 cup red lentils

1 teaspoon cumin seeds

1 teaspoon mustard seeds

1 teaspoon coriander seeds

2 pounds grouper, cut into
   2-ounce pieces

1 cup orange supremes

1 cup fresh cilantro leaves

In a large sauté pan over high heat, combine the onion, garlic, ginger, curry powder and 2 tablespoons of the oil. Cook until the onion begins to color, about 4 minutes. Mix in the spinach and cook until it just wilts, about 5 minutes. Drain any liquid in the pan through a colander. Return the spinach to the pan and mix in the yogurt. Season with salt and set the saag aside.

In a small pot over high heat, combine the citrus zests with enough water to cover and boil for 1 minute. Strain off the water and replace with fresh water. Repeat the process three times.

Transfer the zests to a blender. Add the sugar, lemon juice to taste and 2 tablespoons of the oil. Purée on high speed until very smooth, about 3 minutes. With the motor running, add 3 tablespoons water to emulsify the citrus purée. Season with salt, transfer to a bowl and clean and dry the blender.

Combine the lentils and spices in the clean blender. Blend at high speed until the lentils are reduced to a powder. Transfer the lentils to a flat dish.

Season the grouper with salt, then dredge the fish pieces through the lentil mixture, shaking off the excess.

In a large sauté pan over high heat, sauté the fish in the remaining ¼ cup oil until crisp on all sides, 8 to 10 minutes total.

Arrange the fish on four dinner plates. Place several spoonfuls of the curried spinach and the citrus sauce alongside. Garnish with the citrus segments and the cilantro. Serve immediately.

BRANDADE-CRUSTED ATLANTIC COD
WITH PIPERADE & PARSLEY PURÉE

Cod is a wonderful, flaky fish with great flavor. But it is delicate and loves to fall apart while cooking. I've solved that problem in this traditionally inspired dish with a touch of innovation. I pair the fresh cod with brandade, the classic French salt cod and potato purée. Add in toasted breadcrumbs and the brandade makes a nice crust to protect the fish in the pan and deepen the flavors. Piperade, the traditional Basque slow-cooked sweet pepper stew, further develops the flavors and the parsley purée adds an herbal brightness.

SERVES 4

6 ounces salt cod

2 medium potatoes, peeled and sliced

1 medium onion, diced

¼ cup sliced garlic

7 tablespoons sunflower oil

1 cup white wine

1 cup heavy cream

2 bay leaves

1 cup breadcrumbs

1 tablespoon fresh thyme leaves

sea salt

1½ pounds cod fillets, cut into 6-ounce pieces

½ cup rice flour

1 cup chopped fresh parsley

2 ice cubes

1 teaspoon lemon juice

PIPERADE

6 red peppers

¼ cup shallot confit (see larder)

6 cloves garlic, sliced

1 tablespoon olive oil

1 bay leaf

1 sprig fresh rosemary

½ cup white wine

sea salt

Soak the salt cod in cold water for 1 hour. Discard the water.

Meanwhile, make the piperade: Over a gas flame, char the whole red peppers. Transfer to a medium bowl, cover tightly with plastic wrap and let cool for about 20 minutes. Remove the plastic, pour in enough warm water to cover and peel the peppers under the water. Rinse off the loose peels under running water and slice the roasted peppers.

In a medium pot over medium heat, combine the shallot confit, garlic and olive oil and cook until the garlic just begins to color, about 5 minutes. Add the peppers, herbs and wine and reduce by half. Season with salt and set aside.

In a medium pot over high heat, combine the potatoes, onion, garlic and 2 tablespoons of the sunflower oil. Cook until the onions just begin to color, about 7 minutes. Add the salt cod, wine and enough water to cover. Cook until the water is reduced by three-quarters and the potatoes are very tender, about 1 hour. Add the cream and bay leaves, reduce the heat to low and cook for 10 minutes more. Transfer to the bowl of a mixer with a paddle attachment. Mix on low speed until smooth, about 5 minutes. Add the breadcrumbs and thyme and mix well. The brandade should be as thick as mashed potatoes; add additional breadcrumbs as necessary.

Season the cod with salt. Dredge the tops of the fillets in the rice flour, shaking off the excess. Top each fillet with 3 tablespoons of the brandade, smoothing it with a damp spatula.

In a large sauté pan over high heat, sauté the fillets, brandade side down, in 3 tablespoons of the sunflower oil until golden, about 4 minutes. Carefully turn the fillets over and cook for about 7 minutes more. Keep warm.

In a blender, purée the parsley, ice and remaining 2 tablespoons sunflower oil until very smooth, about 2 minutes. Strain through a fine sieve into a small bowl. Season with salt and stir in the lemon juice.

Spread the parsley purée across the bottom of four plates. Top each with a scoop of the piperade and a cod fillet. Serve immediately.

PETRALE SOLE
WITH SUMMER VEGETABLES & PANISSE

Panisse is a tradition from Marsaille of frites made from chickpea flour. We make our own chickpea flour and one day I tried it for crusting paper-thin fillets of petrale sole—it was fantastic! Here, I've combined both the fish and the panisse in an elegant dish that celebrates summer. A simple sauté of height-of-season vegetables adds an explosion of color and flavor to the dish. The tart aïoli brings the elements together.

SERVES 4

2 cups dry chickpeas, picked through

1 sprig fresh rosemary

sea salt

2 tablespoons sunflower oil, plus more for frying

2 medium summer squash, shaved into ribbons

½ cup fresh beans, shucked (see note, page 137)

½ cup haricots verts, trimmed

½ cup red peppers, julienned

½ cup cherry tomatoes, washed and dried

2 tablespoons olive oil

2 teaspoons lemon juice, plus more to taste

2 pounds petrale sole fillets

½ cup julienned basil leaves

½ cup traditional aïoli (see larder)

In the bowl of a blender, purée the chickpeas to a fine powder, working in batches if necessary. You should have 2½ cups chickpea flour.

In a medium pot over medium heat, combine 2 cups of the chickpea flour with 6 cups water, the rosemary and a pinch of salt. Cook, stirring often, until the mixture thickens and has a glassy appearance, about 30 minutes. Transfer to a baking sheet lined with wax paper. Using a damp spatula, smooth into a ½-inch-thick layer. Cool the tray in the refrigerator for 30 minutes to firm up the panisse.

In a large pot, heat 1 inch of oil to 375°F, as measured by a deep-fry thermometer.

Once firm, cut the panisse into 1-inch squares and fry in small batches until golden. Using a hand strainer, transfer to paper towels to drain and season with salt. Continue until all the panisse is fried.

In a large sauté pan over high heat, sauté the summer squash, beans, haricots verts, red peppers and tomatoes in the olive oil until al dente, about 4 minutes. Season with salt and toss with lemon juice to taste. Set aside.

Season the fillets with salt and dredge on one side through the remaining ½ cup chickpea flour, shaking off the excess. In a large sauté pan over high heat, sauté the fillets, floured side down, in 2 tablespoons sunflower oil until golden, about 3 minutes. Transfer to a warmed platter and drizzle with the 2 teaspoons of lemon juice.

Divide the summer vegetables among four dinner plates. Top each with the fish and panisse. Garnish with the basil and aïoli and serve immediately.

GRILLED SCALLOPS WITH LIME COCONUT SAUCE

I love this dish during the heat of summer as it is both satisfying and light. Scallops pick up an intriguingly smoky aroma on the grill. Their sweet flavor is offset by the tart coconut sauce scented with lime. Cucumbers add a pleasant, cooling crunch.

SERVES 4

1 cup coconut milk

1 tablespoons lime juice

1 tablespoon sliced fresh
    ginger

2 fresh lime leaves

sea salt

1 cup peeled and shaved
    cucumbers

1 tablespoon sunflower oil

1 teaspoon white wine vinegar

12 large scallops, rinsed and
    dried

2 tablespoons ground dried
    wakame seaweed (optional)

In a small pot over high heat, combine the coconut milk, lime juice, ginger and lime leaves and cook until thickened, about 20 minutes. Season with salt and set aside.

In a medium bowl, combine the cucumbers, oil and the vinegar. Season with salt and set aside.

Season the scallops with salt. Grill the scallops over a wood or charcoal flame until lightly charred, about 2 minutes. Turn the scallops over to grill for 1 minute more. Move the scallops to a cool part of the grill to keep warm.

Divide the scallops among four plates. Garnish each serving with the cucumbers, coconut sauce and seaweed, if using. Serve immediately.

GROUND DRIED SEAWEED

Adding small, often imperceptible, layers of seaweed into the background of a dish is a great way to add depth to a range of flavors on the plate. The salty, umami, herbaceous character of seaweed subtly fills in the gaps. The trick is to use just a touch. Add too much and the flavor of a dish becomes decidedly of seaweed. Try grinding a bit into the salt you'll use in soups and broths. A small piece of kombu tossed into a pot of broth serves the same purpose. Dried wakame, while offering the same flavor, is thin enough to be ground into a powder. Or, left whole, wakame adds a pleasant crunch when added at the end of a recipe.

COBIA WRAPPED IN JAMON SERRANO
WITH FRESH BEANS & GRILLED LEMONS

Roasting fish wrapped in a paper-thin layer of jamon Serrano, or spiced dried ham, adds complexity and depth of flavor. The flavor of the fish and ham meld during roasting and the ham picks up a delicate crispness. The fresh braised beans add creaminess and the lemon a burst of acidity that brings together the elements. I add the herbs to the braised beans during the last few minutes of cooking so their vivid flavor is not lost.

SERVES 4

2 cups peeled cardoons, cut into 1-inch lengths
sea salt
1 medium onion, diced
¼ cup roasted garlic (see larder)
1 cup diced carrot
3 tablespoons sunflower oil
2 cups fresh beans (see note, page 137)
1 quart fish or chicken stock (see larder)
2 cups white wine
1 tablespoon lemon zest
2 sprigs fresh savory
2 sprigs fresh thyme
2 sprigs fresh sage
1 lemon, thinly sliced
1½ pounds cobia fillets, cut into 6-ounce portions
1 cup shaved jamon Serrano or other dried ham
2 tablespoons olive oil, plus more for finishing

In small pot over high heat, combine the cardoons and enough water to cover. Season with salt and cook until the cardoons are tender, about 30 minutes. Drain.

In a large pot over high heat, combine the onion, roasted garlic, carrot, cardoons and 2 tablespoons of the sunflower oil. Cook until the onion just begins to color, about 5 minutes. Add the beans, stock and wine and cook until the beans are tender, about 10 minutes. Add the lemon zest and herbs, season with salt and set aside.

Toss the lemons with the remaining 1 tablespoon sunflower oil. Grill the lemon slices over a wood or charcoal fire until lightly charred. Transfer to a platter large enough to hold the cobia fillets.

Wrap the fish fillets in the ham slices, securing with toothpicks if necessary. In a large sauté pan over high heat, sauté the fillets in the olive oil until they begin to brown and the ham is crisp, about 5 minutes per side. Transfer to the platter and top with the grilled lemon slices.

Divide the bean mixture among four large bowls. Top with the fillets and grilled lemon slices. Drizzle with olive oil and serve immediately.

COBIA

Red wine with fish? Perhaps not with some delicate types, but certainly with this firm, meaty fish. Cobia's steak-like texture and clean flavor allow it to hold its own when paired with medium-bodied red wines like Pinot Noir or Sangiovese. I often use it in dishes that mimic roasted meat, or better yet that combine the fish with meat elements. So as far as wine pairing goes, cobia does not play by the rules. To our delight, it makes its own.

BROOK TROUT
WITH GOLD BEETS & BUCKWHEAT NOODLES

Buckwheat noodles, or *soba* in Japanese, are the epitome of fall flavor to me. Their haunting toasty flavor seems to capture the image of golden leaves falling from trees. Here, I've used the noodles as a starting point for a simple grilled trout dish. The sweet, buttery golden beets add wonderful color and richness, while the smoky grilled leeks add a hint of campfire aromas.

SERVES 4

2 large leeks
1 pound gold beets, peeled
  and sliced
¼ cup unsalted butter
1 pound buckwheat noodles
2 tablespoons hazelnut oil
2 tablespoons sherry vinegar
4 brook trout, boned
sea salt
2 tablespoons sunflower oil
3 tablespoons lemon juice
  or to taste
toasted hazelnuts, for garnish
1 tablespoon pickled ginger,
  julienned (see larder)

Trim and discard the green tops from the leeks. Cut the leeks into quarters, leaving the root ends attached. Wash in several changes of water until very clean.

In a medium saucepan over high heat, boil the leeks and beets in salted water until tender, about 20 minutes. Drain in a colander, reserve the leeks, and return the beets to the pot. Add the butter and return the pot to the stove on low heat to melt the butter and keep warm. Check the beets for seasoning and adjust if necessary.

In a large saucepan over high heat, boil the noodles in salted water until tender, about 6 minutes. Drain in a colander, return to the saucepan and season with the hazelnut oil and vinegar.

Season the trout with salt and dress lightly with the sunflower oil. Grill the trout and leeks over a wood or charcoal fire or in a grill pan over high heat until lightly charred, about 2 minutes. Transfer to a warm platter and season with the lemon juice.

Divide the trout among four warmed plates. Top each with the leeks, beets, noodles, toasted hazelnuts and pickled ginger. Serve immediately.

WILD SALMON WITH CHANTERELLES & BRAISED CELERY

Wild salmon's robust flavor and texture can stand up to full throttle, red wine–focused presentations. Wild mushrooms, cooked slowly with rich goose liver butter, provide just such an opportunity. Braised celery adds lightness to the dish, while the sturdy Cabernet Franc sauce balances the elements.

SERVES 4

2 bay leaves

2 tablespoons black
  peppercorns

1 medium onion, diced

¼ cup diced celery plus 8 ribs
  celery, peeled and cut into
  2-inch pieces

3 tablespoons sunflower oil

3 cups Cabernet Franc

2 cups chicken or beef stock
  (see larder)

4 tablespoons unsalted butter,
  softened

3 cups vegetable stock
  (see larder)

1 tablespoon white wine
  vinegar

1 cup white wine

2 sprigs fresh sage

sea salt

½ cup fresh celery leaves

2 cups chanterelles, black
  trumpets or other wild
  mushrooms

4 tablespoons goose liver
  butter (see larder)

lemon juice to taste

2 pounds wild salmon fillets,
  skin removed

Place a 7-inch square of cheesecloth on a clean work surface. Place the bay leaves and 1 tablespoon of the peppercorns in the center, draw up the sides and tie together to form a sachet.

In a medium saucepan over high heat, cook the onion and diced celery in 2 tablespoons of the oil until the onion begins to color, about 4 minutes. Add the wine, chicken stock and sachet, reduce the heat to a simmer and cook until reduced by half. Keep warm.

In a heavy-bottomed braising pan, cook the celery pieces in 2 tablespoons of the butter over high heat until golden, about 7 minutes. Add the vegetable stock, the remaining 1 tablespoon peppercorns, the vinegar, white wine and sage and reduce by three-quarters. Remove from the heat and stir in the celery leaves and the remaining 2 tablespoons butter until the butter is fully melted. Season with salt and keep warm.

In a medium sauté pan over medium-high heat, sauté the mushrooms in 2 tablespoons of the goose liver butter until they begin to brown, about 7 minutes. Remove from the heat and stir in the remaining 2 tablespoons goose liver butter. Season with salt and lemon juice.

Cut the salmon fillets into 8-ounce portions and season on both sides with salt. In a large sauté pan over high heat, sauté the salmon, skin side up, in the remaining 1 tablespoon oil until browned and crisp, about 3 minutes. Reduce the heat to low, turn the salmon over and cook the second side, about 3 minutes more. Remove the fish from the heat.

Divide the celery and mushrooms among four warmed plates. Top with the salmon and garnish with the sauce. Serve immediately.

SALSIFY

With its creamy texture and sweet, earthy flavor, salsify is endearing. Its traditional preparation calls for poaching the peeled roots gently in milk scented with nutmeg. Then they are tossed in butter to serve. It's a method that's hard to beat as it showcases the root's delicious, comforting flavor. I keep a few lemon halves handy to rub down the roots as I peel them, as they oxidize quickly.

ROASTED STURGEON WITH SALSIFY & BEETS

I love sturgeon; while clean in flavor, its texture is firm and moist, allowing the fish to stand up to bold flavors. In this dish, salsify adds substance, beets and blood orange add strong sweet-and-sour elements and smoked salt adds complexity.

SERVES 4

2 large red beets
1 cup red wine vinegar
1 tablespoon salt, plus more
    for seasoning
2 tablespoons honey
2 pieces star anise
¼ cup basic vinaigrette
    (see larder)
5 cups salsify, peeled
1 tablespoon lemon juice, plus
    more for seasoning
1½ pounds sturgeon fillet,
    cut into 6-ounce portions
1 tablespoon smoked salt
    (see larder)
3 tablespoons duck fat or
    butter, melted
2 blood oranges, sliced

In a medium pot over high heat, cook the beets in 1 quart water with the vinegar, salt, honey and star anise until tender, about 30 minutes. Remove the beets from the pot and cool for 4 minutes. Peel and slice the beets thinly on a mandolin. Dress with the vinaigrette, season with salt and set aside.

Meanwhile, in a medium pot, boil the salsify in salted water with the lemon juice until just tender, about 20 minutes. Strain through a colander and set aside.

Preheat the oven to 450°F.

Season the sturgeon with the smoked salt on all sides. Place the fillets and salsify on a roasting pan and dress with the duck fat. Roast until the fish is firm to the touch and heated through, 18 to 20 minutes. Remove from the oven and season with lemon juice.

Divide the fish and salsify between four dinner plates. Garnish with the beets and blood orange slices and serve immediately.

COD ROASTED IN SAVOY CABBAGE
WITH MUSHROOMS & BRAISED LENTILS

Savoy, or crinkled-leaf cabbage, is the best choice for roasting here, as it lends a sweet, savory aroma to the cod. It is perfect for an elegant winter dinner. The earthiness of braised lentils and mushrooms further ground the dish. A simple beurre blanc, scented in the end with truffles if you're lucky enough to have them, makes the dish fit for a celebration.

SERVES 4

¾ cup diced onion

¼ cup diced celery

1 tablespoon minced garlic

1 cup (2 sticks) plus 3 tablespoons unsalted butter, softened

2 cups plus 2 tablespoons white wine

2 tablespoons heavy cream

6 sprigs fresh thyme

sea salt

1 tablespoon black truffles, minced (optional)

1 tablespoon black truffle oil

3 cups mushrooms, sliced

2 cups cooked French lentils

freshly ground black pepper

1 head savoy cabbage

1½ pounds cod fillets, cut into 6-ounce pieces

¼ cup duck fat or unsalted butter

Preheat the oven to 450°F.

In a small saucepan over high heat, cook ¼ cup of the onion, the celery and garlic in 1 tablespoon of the butter until the onion begins to brown, about 4 minutes. Add 2 cups of the wine and fully reduce. Remove from the heat and stir in the cream and 2 sprigs of the thyme. Fold in the remaining 1 cup butter, a tablespoon at a time, stirring constantly, until melted. Season with salt, then strain the butter sauce through a fine sieve. Return the sauce to the pot and add the truffles, if using, and truffle oil. Keep warm.

In a large sauté pan over high heat, cook the remaining ½ cup onion in the remaining 2 tablespoons butter until the onions just begin to brown. Stir in the sliced mushrooms and cook until they begin to brown, about 15 minutes. Add the remaining 2 tablespoons wine and scrape the bottom of the pan to loosen the browned bits. Set aside 3 tablespoons of the mushrooms. Decrease the temperature to low and stir in the cooked lentils, remaining 4 sprigs of thyme and 1 tablespoon of the reserved truffle butter sauce. Cook until the lentils are warmed through. Season with salt and pepper.

Using a paring knife, cut out the heart of the cabbage. Peel whole leaves off—depending on their size, you will need 8 to 12. Blanch the leaves in boiling salted water until pliable, about 15 seconds. Drain and cool.

Season the cod with salt. Top each fillet with a small spoonful of the reserved mushrooms. Tightly wrap the fillets in the cabbage leaves, securing with toothpicks if necessary. Place on a baking sheet and dot the tops with the duck fat. Bake until the cabbage begins to brown and the fish is cooked through.

Place a scoop of lentils in the center of four warmed plates. Top with the fish, then drizzle the fish with the truffle butter sauce. Serve immediately.

POACHED LOBSTER
WITH JAUNE D'DOUB CARROT GRATIN

I love this dish for its explosion of flavors and riot of colors. It amazes me that such a brightly flavored dish is not only possible in the heart of winter, but is at its peak! Lobster makes an elegant dish on its own. Here, it is poached gently in butter, which keeps it tender. The delicate leaves of mâche, the heartiest of all winter greens, are harvested at our farm from underneath the snow. When the world is frozen over and barren, the mâche is at its tender best.

SERVES 4

JAUNE DE DOUB GRATIN

1 pound Jaune de Doub
  carrots, thinly sliced

1 medium onion, finely
  julienned

2 tablespoons minced garlic

¼ cup heavy cream

¼ cup milk

sea salt

3 tablespoons julienned
  grapefruit zest

2 tablespoons sugar

2 tablespoons plus 2 cups
  fresh grapefruit juice

2 tablespoons plus ¼ cup
  heavy cream

2 cups (4 sticks) unsalted
  butter, softened

3 whole lobsters, removed
  from shells

sea salt

½ cup lobster stock or water

2 cups mâche

2 tablespoons basic
  vinaigrette (see larder)

1 cup red grapefruit segments

First, make the carrot gratin: Preheat the oven to 400°F. In a medium bowl, combine the carrots, onion, garlic, cream and milk. Season with salt and toss well. Pour into a 7-inch square baking dish and, with a spatula, press the mixture down to remove any air and to level the top. Bake, covered, in the oven until the cream begins to boil, about 30 minutes. Lower the temperature to 325°F and bake until the cream has evaporated and the carrots are very tender, about 45 minutes more. Remove from the oven and uncover. Compress the gratin using the back side of a spatula, then cut into 1½-inch squares. Set aside.

In a small pot, pour enough water over the zest to cover and boil for 1 minute. Strain the zest through a sieve, discarding the water. Return the zest to the pot and repeat the process until the zest is only slightly bitter, about four times total. Once the zest is no longer bitter, combine it in the pot with the sugar and 2 tablespoons of the grapefruit juice. Boil for 2 minutes and set aside.

In a small pot over high heat, boil the remaining 2 cups grapefruit juice until reduced by three-quarters. Stir in 2 tablespoons of the cream and remove from the heat. Add half the butter and whisk continuously until fully melted. Season with salt and add half the candied grapefruit zest. Set aside.

Cut the lobster tails into ½-inch-thick slices and season with salt. In a medium pot over high heat, combine the remaining butter, the ¼ cup cream, and lobster stock and season with salt. Add the lobster, reduce the heat to a bare simmer and cook until warmed through. Remove from the heat and let stand for 4 minutes.

In a small bowl, mix the mâche and vinaigrette. Season with salt and toss well.

Place two squares of the gratin on each of four plates. Divide the lobster among the plates and top with the butter sauce. Garnish with the candied grapefruit, the fresh grapefruit segments and mâche. Serve immediately.

WILD FORAGED

THROUGHOUT THE YEAR THERE ARE ALWAYS EDIBLE, WILD HERBS AVAILABLE.

EARLY IN THE SPRING, DANDELIONS AND NETTLES ARE AT THEIR PEAK.

LATER IN THE YEAR THE LAMB'S QUARTERS AND MALLOW ARE DELICIOUS.

AS THE YEAR TURNS COLDER, I LOOK FOR CHICKWEED AND WILD LETTUCE.

NOW THAT I KNOW WHICH PLANTS TO LOOK FOR, I'M ALWAYS AMAZED TO SEE

SO MUCH DELICIOUS FOOD LITERALLY UNDERFOOT.

GNOCCHI WITH THE FIRST WILD HERBS OF THE YEAR

While on a trip to the Camino Valley in Italy, I had a dish of gnocchi with nettles and Gorgonzola; it was how they served the first greens of the year. I loved the idea and here I've adapted it to the Front Range of the Rockies by using the first edible wild herbs that peak up through the snow. But you can use any combination of fresh wild herbs.

SERVES 4

3 cups all-purpose flour
1 cup fresh goat cheese
2 large eggs
2 teaspoons sea salt, plus more for seasoning
2 quarts whey (see note)
2 cups chopped wild herbs, such as mallow,

wild lettuce, nettle or dandelion
¼ cup roasted garlic (see larder)
3 tablespoon white wine
¼ cup heavy cream
½ teaspoon freshly grated nutmeg
blue cheese, crumbled

CHEESE AND WHEY

After making a few batches of fresh goat cheese and ricotta I found myself swimming in the leftover whey. What to do with it all? The clever idea in this dish is to use whey in lieu of water for boiling the pasta, which adds extra flavor to the gnocchi. Use water with a dash of heavy cream as a substitute. I use whey for poaching chicken and turkey breasts as well.

Avalanche Cheese Company in Colorado has been wowing us and winning awards with their cheeses for a few years. Their Midnight Blue goat cheese is perfect for this dish.

In a medium bowl, combine the flour, cheese, eggs and salt and work into a dough. Transfer to a floured work surface and knead until smooth, adding a little extra flour if necessary. Form the dough into a long cigar shape, about ¾ inch in diameter. Slice crosswise into ½-inch-thick slices. Using a fork, push down on a slice of the dough and roll the dough off of the fork to form the gnocchi. Continue until all of the dough is used up.

Bring the whey to a boil in a large pot. Season with salt. Working in batches, boil the gnocchi until firm, about 5 minutes. Using a slotted spoon, transfer to a tray to cool. Repeat until the gnocchi are all cooked.

In a medium saucepan, combine the herbs, roasted garlic, wine, cream and nutmeg. Cook until the herbs are wilted and the cream has begun to thicken, about 6 minutes. Season with salt, then add the gnocchi and simmer until warmed through. Add a little of the whey used for cooking the gnocchi if the sauce is too thick.

Divide the gnocchi among four warmed bowls. Top with crumbles of the cheese and serve immediately.

FORAGED ASPARAGUS WITH MOREL FRICASSEE

Throughout the farms of our region, asparagus grows wild along the banks of the irrigation ditches and canals lining the fields. Often, I'll skip lunch while working in the fields if there is a promising patch nearby—choosing to sit on the banks and graze in the spring sun is always a better option. For the asparagus in this dish, I prefer the fattest stalks possible as they are the sweetest. Good foraged morels often have a remnant smoky quality left over from their growth in areas of forest fires.

SERVES 4

2 cups fresh morels, rinsed
and dried

1 medium onion, minced

5 tablespoons unsalted butter,
softened

3 tablespoons vegetable stock
(see larder)

1 small piece of kombu
seaweed

sea salt and freshly ground
black pepper

4 baby carrots, trimmed and
halved lengthwise

1 small spring onion, cut into
quarters

1 young green garlic clove,
minced

1 cup heavy cream

3 sprigs fresh thyme plus
1 tablespoon leaves

1 pound asparagus, peeled

lemon juice

1 tablespoon lemon zest

In a medium pan over high heat, sauté the mushrooms and onion in 2 tablespoons of the butter, stirring often, until the onions begin to color, about 7 minutes. Reduce the heat to low, add the stock and kombu and simmer until the stock has evaporated, about 2 minutes more. Season with salt and pepper.

Meanwhile, in a second pan over medium heat, sauté the carrots in 1 tablespoon of the butter until just tender, about 4 minutes. Add the spring onion and garlic and cook for 3 minutes more. Season with salt and pepper and stir in the mushrooms and cream. Bring to a boil until thickened slightly, about 5 minutes. Remove from the heat, add the thyme and keep warm.

In a large pan over high heat, sauté the asparagus in the remaining 2 tablespoons butter until it just begins to brown, about 4 minutes. Season with salt, lemon juice, and the lemon zest.

Divide the asparagus among four plates. Top with the morel fricassee, garnish with the thyme leaves and serve immediately.

Overleaf: Foraged asparagus with morel fricassee and Morel mushrooms

CRISP RISOTTO CAKES
WITH DANDELION GREENS

For much of the year, dandelion greens are too bitter to eat. But early in the spring, before winter has lost the last of its icy grip, the greens are at their best. Here, I've included them in a simple risotto. Salty ingredients have the ability to tame bitterness so I've added salted lemons towards that end. The tart confit baby leeks adds brightness to the dish.

SERVES 4

1 medium onion, minced

¼ cup minced garlic

5 tablespoons sunflower oil

2 cups Arborio rice

1 quart vegetable stock
    (see larder)

3 cups white wine

6 bay leaves

½ cup grated Gruyère cheese

1 cup toasted breadcrumbs

1 tablespoon peppercorns

2 cups diced leeks

2 tablespoons olive oil

2 cups chopped dandelion
    greens

½ cup julienned salted lemons
    (see larder)

½ cup soft ripened cheese,
    such as MouCo Camembert

In a large saucepan over high heat, cook the onion and garlic in 2 tablespoons sunflower oil, stirring often, until the onions just begin to color, about 4 minutes. Add the rice and cook, stirring constantly, for 1 minute. Pour in 2 cups of the stock, 1 cup of the wine and 4 bay leaves. Cook, stirring often, until the liquid is nearly absorbed. Repeat until all the stock is used up, about 30 minutes total. Season with salt and cook until the grains are al dente. Remove from the heat and fold in the Gruyère.

Line a baking sheet with wax paper. Spread the cooked risotto over the paper in a ½-inch-thick layer. Cool the risotto in the refrigerator until it sets, about 2 hours. Using a 2-inch diameter cutter, cut the risotto into rounds. Repack and flatten the scraps to use up all of the risotto. Dredge the risotto cakes in the breadcrumbs on both sides. Set aside.

Using a 7-inch square of cheesecloth, form a bundle or sachet with the remaining 2 bay leaves and the peppercorns. Place in a small saucepan with the leeks and the remaining 2 cups wine. Cook over high heat until the wine has fully reduced, about 20 minutes. Remove from the heat and add the olive oil. Season with salt and mix well.

Meanwhile, working in batches in a large sauté pan over high heat, sauté the cakes in the remaining 3 tablespoons sunflower oil until golden on both sides, about 8 minutes. Set aside on a platter.

In a large sauté pan over high heat, cook the dandelion greens and the leeks until the greens wilt. Add the lemons and mix well.

Divide the risotto cakes among four plates. Top with the dandelion-leek mixture. Garnish with the soft cheese and serve immediately.

BITTER HERBS
For bitter herbs, like dandelion, harvest them when it is very cold outside as they are sweetest then. Once they are chopped and cooked, they excel as a stuffing or in sauces.

CRISPY THISTLE ROOT TEMPURA WITH DASHI

Confounded by the stubborn thistle that grows in some of our fields, I decided to search for a way to turn this "lemon" into the proverbial lemonade. The young, tender shoots of the thistle make an excellent, crisp tempura. Its long, thin delicate shape lends itself to a great garnish for other dishes, too.

SERVES 4

1 cup vegetable stock (see larder)	sea salt
1 small piece of kombu seaweed	sunflower oil
1 teaspoon bonito flakes	1 cup rice flour
1 teaspoon sugar	½ cup soda water or light beer
rice vinegar to taste	4 ounces thistle roots, cleaned and trimmed

In a small saucepan over medium-high heat, combine the stock, kombu, bonito and sugar. Season with vinegar and salt and simmer for 5 minutes. Chill the dashi broth in the refrigerator at least 2 hours or overnight.

In a large pot, heat 2 inches of the oil to 375°F, as measured on a deep-fry thermometer.

In a medium bowl, combine the rice flour, a pinch of salt and the soda water. Dip the thistle roots into the batter and fry in the oil until golden, about 2 minutes. Drain the roots on paper towels and season with salt.

Place the tempura on a serving platter. Pour the chilled dashi into a serving bowl and place alongside. Serve immediately.

GRILLED PORCINI & DUCK LIVERS WITH RICE

Soon after the summer rains begin, Boletus mushrooms appear high in the mountains. Foraging mushrooms makes for a perfect excuse to quietly wander through the woods, which is what I do each weekend with our family after the farmer's market. This dish is replete with rich smoky flavors, reminding me of camping high in the Rocky Mountains.

SERVES 4

1 cup wild rice	½ pound porcini mushrooms, washed and quartered
sea salt	
½ cup goose liver butter (see larder)	½ pound duck livers, soaked and dried
½ cup chopped lovage	1 cup shallot confit (see larder)
1 ice cube	
½ cup plus 2 tablespoons sunflower oil	

In a medium pot over high heat, combine the rice with 5 cups water and season with salt. Boil until tender, about 45 minutes. Strain through a colander and return to the pot. Add 2 tablespoons of the goose liver butter and mix well. Season with salt.

In a blender, purée the lovage, ice, ½ cup of the oil and a pinch of salt on high speed until smooth, about 2 minutes. Taste for seasoning and adjust if necessary.

In a large pan over high heat, sauté the porcinis in the remaining 2 tablespoons oil until golden, about 2 minutes. Turn the mushrooms over in the pan, add the duck livers and cook until the livers are browned and cooked through. Reduce the heat to low and add the remaining 6 tablespoons goose liver butter and the shallot confit. Season with salt and cook just until the butter melts and the shallots are warmed through.

Spread the lovage oil on four dinner plates. Top with the mushrooms, livers and shallots and several spoonfuls of rice. Serve immediately.

QUINOA SPÄTZLE WITH LAMB'S QUARTERS

Quinoa, a delicately nutty grain, is related to the warm-season wild herb, lamb's quarters, which has a spinach-like flavor. So, it was not too long a leap to combine them here. Harvested young, lamb's quarters is quite tender. Baby spinach can be substituted.

SERVES 4

2 cups cooked quinoa

4 cups all-purpose flour

2 cups whole milk

3 large eggs

¼ cup minced roasted garlic (see larder)

sea salt

2 medium onions, peeled and quartered

1 tablespoon sunflower oil

fruit wood, for smoking

3 tablespoons unsalted butter, softened

1 cup red grapes, halved

¼ cup hazelnuts, toasted

2 cups chopped fresh lamb's quarters

verjus to taste

In a medium bowl, combine the quinoa, flour, milk, eggs, garlic and a pinch of salt.

In a large pot over high heat, bring 1 gallon of salted water to a boil, then reduce to a simmer. Set a large-holed colander over, but not touching, the water. Working in small batches, push the quinoa dough through the holes of the colander with a rubber spatula. Cook for 3 to 4 minutes, until the spätzle floats to the surface, stirring gently to prevent sticking. Transfer to a second colander and rinse with cool water. Repeat until the batter is used up. Set aside.

In a small bowl, mix the onions with 2 teaspoons salt and dress in the oil. Smoke in a smoker, according to the manufacturer's directions. Alternatively, roast the onions in a 450°F oven until they begin to brown, about 10 minutes. Julienne and set aside.

In a large pan over high heat, sauté the spätzle in the butter until golden, about 3 minutes. Stir in the onions, grapes, hazelnuts and lamb's quarters and sauté for 3 minutes. Season with verjus and salt and serve immediately.

JACK BE LITTLE PUMPKIN & POLENTA SOUFFLÉ

Roasted heirloom pumpkin and a ragout of mushrooms fill a soufflé dish, which is topped with a soufflé made from polenta. With the addition of Parmesan and sautéed Brussels sprouts, this entrée is a showstopper. The Jack Be Little pumpkins are themselves a fun stand-in for a basic soufflé dish. Other possible varieties include acorn, delicata and dumpling squashes. If those are not available, butternut squash makes a fine substitute.

SERVES 4

8 Jack Be Little pumpkins
3 tablespoons sunflower oil
sea salt and freshly ground
  black pepper
2 cups sliced mushrooms
1 medium onion, sliced
¼ cup minced garlic
2 tablespoons white wine
2 tablespoons softened butter,
  plus more for sautéeing
6 sprigs fresh thyme
1¼ cups cornmeal or polenta
1½ cups whole milk
4 bay leaves
½ cup heavy cream
½ teaspoon freshly grated
  nutmeg
4 large eggs, at room
  temperature, separated
3 cups Brussels sprouts,
  separated into leaves

Preheat the oven to 450°F.

Cut the tops from the pumpkins. Remove and discard the seeds and pulp from the cavities. Dress the pumpkins and tops with 1 tablespoon of the oil, salt and pepper. Place on a baking sheet and roast in the oven until tender and beginning to brown, about 15 minutes. Set aside to cool.

In a large sauté pan over high heat, combine the mushrooms, onion, garlic and the remaining 2 tablespoons oil. Cook, stirring occasionally, until the vegetables begin to brown, about 15 minutes. Add the wine and scrape the pan to remove any browned bits. Add the butter and thyme, season with salt and set aside off the heat.

In a medium saucepan over medium heat, combine the cornmeal, 1 quart water and milk, stirring very well to hydrate the cornmeal. Bring to a boil then lower the heat to low. Add the bay leaves and cook, stirring often, until the mixture is very thick and the cornmeal is very soft. Add the cream and nutmeg, season with salt and stir well. Transfer the polenta to a large bowl and let cool. Add the egg yolks and mix well to combine.

In a medium bowl, whisk the egg whites until soft peaks form. Fold the whites into the polenta mixture in thirds without overmixing—a few loose streaks of egg white is fine.

Divide the mushrooms and onions among the roasted pumpkins, filling the cavities. Top with the polenta mixture until the pumpkins are full. Bake until the polenta is set and the soufflés have risen, about 15 minutes.

Meanwhile, in a large sauté pan over high heat, sauté the Brussels sprouts in a bit of butter until the leaves just begin to color, about 6 minutes. Season with salt.

Divide the pumpkins among four dinner plates. Garnish with the Brussels sprouts and pumpkin tops and serve immediately.

FARMER'S CHEESE
WITH APPLE BUTTER & WALNUTS

Old farms abound in our region. While many of them are no longer producing, their old forgotten apple trees are. Foraged apples lend an outstanding complexity for apple butter. While most are not pretty—often scarred and misshapen—they have real taste. Save the whey from the farmer's cheese to use for the the gnocchi on page 188.

SERVES 4

1 pound foraged apples	2 tablespoons lemon juice
sea salt	or white vinegar
1 cinnamon stick	2 tablespoons heavy
(optional)	cream
sugar	¼ cup toasted walnuts
4 cups whole milk	grilled sourdough bread

Preheat the oven to 300°F.

In a large Dutch oven set over high heat, bring the apples with 1 cup water and ½ teaspoon salt to a boil. Reduce the heat to medium and cook until very soft and all the water has evaporated, about 45 minutes. Purée in a blender until very smooth, about 2 minutes. Return to the pot and add the cinnamon stick, if desired. Bake, stirring every 30 minutes, until thickened, about 3 hours. Season the apple butter with sugar; it will keep, covered, in the fridge for 3 weeks.

Meanwhile, in a saucepan over high heat, bring the milk to a boil. Remove from the heat and add the lemon juice, stirring once to combine. Curds will quickly form in the milk. Let cool, about 15 minutes, after which the curds should have separated from the whey. Using a hand strainer, transfer the curds to a colander lined with cheesecloth to drain for 20 minutes. Place in a bowl and add the cream, season with salt and mix well.

Place the warm apple butter in a serving bowl. Place the cheese in a second bowl and garnish with the walnuts. Serve with the bread.

LAMB SHOULDER
CONFIT WITH SUMAC JUS

Sumac is a traditional spice in Lebanese cuisine and grows wild in hedges and woods throughout the United States. There are two types of sumac that grow wild in the U.S., the edible one with red seeds and the poisonous one with white seeds. The spice comes from a red powdery coating on the seeds. Sumac's flavor is tart and here I use it as a replacement for wine in a sauce for lamb.

SERVES 4

2 pounds lamb shoulder	1 cup plain yogurt
sea salt	freshly ground black
1 quart duck or pork fat	pepper
1 orange, halved	2 cups beef or lamb stock
1 cinnamon stick	(see larder)
4 cardamom pods	1 sprig fresh rosemary
1 cup grated cucumber	1 tablespoon sumac

Preheat the oven to 200°F.

Season the lamb with salt. In a Dutch oven set over medium heat, combine the lamb, fat, orange, cinnamon and cardamom. Cook until the fat is melted and begins to simmer, about 10 minutes. Cover the pan and place in the oven until the lamb is very tender, about 6 hours. Remove from the oven to a warm place.

Meanwhile, place the cucumber in a medium bowl and season heavily with salt. Marinate the cucumber in the salt until it sweats, about 20 minutes. Working in handfuls, wring the liquid out of the cucumber, then rinse the cucumber and pat dry. Add the yogurt, season with salt and pepper and mix well.

In a small saucepan over medium heat, cook the stock, rosemary and sumac until reduced by half. Season with salt and pepper.

Divide the lamb among four plates. Top each with the sumac jus and garnish with the yogurt sauce. Serve immediately.

LATKES WITH SMOKED TROUT & WINTER WATERCRESS

Just below our farmhouse runs a spring-fed stream. Along its banks grows a dense stand of watercress as thick as a carpet. On morning strolls in early winter, I'll often harvest a pail full. I love the bite of watercress paired with smoked trout and created this dish to showcase the two. The latkes are as simple as it gets and delicious, too. Both the brine and fish need to chill for a few hours, so you can make the brine the day before and let the fish marinate the next morning.

SERVES 4

sea salt

2 teaspoons sugar

2 leaves bay laurel

1 teaspoon celery seeds

1 teaspoon freshly ground
  black pepper

4 Brook trout fillets, boned
  and trimmed

2 cups ice

2 large baking potatoes

2 tablespoons sunflower oil

½ cup crème fraîche

1 tablespoon freshly grated
  horseradish

2 teaspoons champagne
  vinegar

2 cups watercress

1 tablespoon basic vinaigrette
  (see larder)

In a small saucepan over high heat, bring 2 cups water with 3 tablespoons salt, the sugar and spices to a boil. Transfer to the fridge to chill for 2 hours.

In a container large enough to hold the fillets flat, combine the fish and brine. Marinate in the refrigerator for 4 hours.

Lay the ice in a thin layer in a flat heatproof container. Top with the fish and place in a smoker to smoke per the manufacturer's directions. Remove the trout from the ice and chill until cold, about 30 minutes. Alternatively, grill or sauté the fish until just warmed through, about 5 minutes.

In a medium pot over high heat, boil the potatoes in salted water until they can be pierced with a sharp knife to the center. Immediately run them under cold water to stop the cooking. When cool enough to handle, grate the potatoes using a box grater and season with salt. Because the potato will be very sticky, use wet hands to form into 2-inch cakes with flat tops and bottoms.

In a large sauté pan over high heat and working in batches, sauté the cakes in the oil until golden and crisp, about 7 minutes. Turn over and cook until the second side is crisp, about 5 minutes more. Transfer to paper towels to drain.

In a small bowl, combine the crème fraiche, horseradish and vinegar. Season with salt and mix well. In another small bowl, combine the watercress and vinaigrette. Season with salt and toss well.

Divide the latkes among four plates. Using a fork, break the trout fillets into rough chunks. Place atop the latkes and add a small spoonful of the crème fraîche. Garnish with the watercress and serve immediately.

COOKING TIP

The best latkes are crisp on the outside with fluffy, light interiors. Relying on eggs and other binders to hold the cakes together results in heavy latkes. It turns out that potatoes need nothing to bind them if they are cooked to the magic temperature of 147°F, when the starch in the potato is fully cooked but still very sticky. I mean VERY sticky. The grated potato will stick to itself to form a cake that can be sautéed in butter to a light, delicious crispness. Cooked to a higher temperature, the potato begins to fall apart (which is what you want for mashed potatoes). At lower temperatures, the potato is still raw and will oxidize once grated.

SMOKED WILD TURKEY FARRO
WITH HAWTHORN BERRIES

Wild turkey is not the same as the domesticated bird we are used to. It has an assertive flavor and can dry out easily when roasting. I take both of these qualities into account in this recipe by making a slow-cooked farro using chunks of the turkey, which is cooked gently in broth to yield a moist bird. (If using domesticated turkey, treat it the same as its wild cousin.) Only after the snows have begun falling at our farm do we begin to harvest from the hawthorn trees, making hawthorn berries the last of the wild foods harvested each year. Rose hips or cranberries make fine substitutes.

SERVES 4

1 medium onion, diced

3 cloves garlic, minced

1 leek, diced

2 tablespoons sunflower oil

2 cups farro

1 quart chicken or turkey
   stock, plus more (see larder)

1 cup white wine

sea salt

freshly grated nutmeg to taste

½ cup heavy cream

1 pound wild turkey, cut into
   bite-sized pieces

6 black peppercorns

1 bay leaf

2 cups hawthorn berries

2 cups red wine

In a large saucepan over high heat, combine the onion, garlic, leek and oil. Cook, stirring often, until the onions begin to color, about 5 minutes. Add the farro, stock and wine and reduce the heat to medium. Cook, stirring often, until the farro is tender, about 45 minutes.

Season the farro with salt and nutmeg, then add the cream and turkey. Reduce the heat to low and cook until the turkey is tender, about 20 minutes, adding more stock if it evaporates.

Place a 7-inch square of cheesecloth on a clean work surface. Place the peppercorns and bay leaf in the center. Draw up the corners and tie them to form a sachet. Place in a small saucepan over high heat with the hawthorn berries and wine and cook until reduced by half. Discard the sachet and pass the mixture through a fine sieve, pressing firmly to extract the meat of the berries. Discard the seeds. Season with salt and stir well.

Divide the farro among four warmed bowls. Top with the hawthorn purée and serve immediately.

DESSERTS

ALL GOOD THINGS MUST COME TO AN END. FORTUNATELY FOR US THAT ENDING
INCLUDES GREAT DESSERTS. THE SEASON'S HARVEST IS ALWAYS THE STARTING
POINT. IN FACT, IT IS THE FOCAL POINT. EACH DESSERT IS A CELEBRATION OF
WHAT WE HAVE THAT IS WONDERFUL IN THE MOMENT. NEXT COME ELEGANT,
REGAL TEXTURES AND THEN A DASH OF WHIMSY AT THE END.

VANILLA PUDDING
WITH CANDIED LOVAGE & STRAWBERRIES

Mara des Bois are the most vividly flavored of all strawberries—they explode with sweet, intense flavor. Here, I've paired them with a rich, yet delicate vanilla pudding and candied lovage. Lovage, a celery cousin, was historically used as a candy with delicious effect. It provides an interesting counterpoint to the strawberries.

SERVES 6

1¾ cups sugar
4 drops lemon juice
1 cup lovage leaves with
    thin stems
1 tablespoon tapioca flour
1½ cups whole milk
½ cup heavy cream
½ teaspoon molasses
1 vanilla bean, split and
    scraped
pinch of freshly grated nutmeg
2 cups Mara des Bois
    strawberries

In a small saucepan over high heat, bring 1 cup sugar with ¼ cup water and the lemon juice to a boil for 1 minute. Remove from the heat and stir in the lovage to separate the leaves in the syrup. Let cool.

Place ¼ cup sugar in a small bowl. Working with one leaf at a time, remove the lovage from the syrup, wiping away the excess. Lightly dredge the leaf in the dry sugar, shaking away any excess. Place on wax paper to dry. Repeat until all of the leaves are coated.

In a medium, heavy-bottomed saucepan over medium heat, combine the tapioca flour, milk, cream, the remaining ½ cup sugar, the molasses, vanilla and nutmeg, whisking well. Cook, stirring constantly, until the pudding thickens. Divide among six dessert bowls and cool thoroughly in the refrigerator until set, about 3 hours. (Cover each bowl with plastic wrap if the puddings will be held in the fridge longer to prevent the tops from drying.)

Top the puddings with the strawberries and the lovage leaves. Serve immediately.

STRAWBERRIES
Ripe strawberries, eaten warmed by the gentle sun of early June are magical. They explode with flavor. We grow thousands of strawberry plants each year. It's a good thing because I'm often heard saying, "One for the guests, one for me..." as I harvest. My favorite varieties are mara des bois and honeoye.

Overleaf: Strawberry and rhubarb tart masquerading as a pizza, in process and cooked

APRICOT, LAVENDER & WHITE CHOCOLATE CRISP

Apricots vary from sweet to tart, depending on the season and often between fruits. I developed this recipe as a way of getting a consistently perfect apricot crisp. White chocolate plays the subtle role of balancing the apricots' sweetness along with creating a velvety texture. I've added a touch of lavender, which adds indulgence to this dish.

SERVES 6

1 cup all-purpose flour
1 cup plus 3 tablespoons sugar
1 large egg
3 tablespoons unsalted butter, melted
pinch of sea salt
pinch of baking powder
1 pound apricots, pitted and sliced
2 to 4 ounces chopped white chocolate
2 tablespoons lavender
1¼ cups heavy cream

Preheat the oven to 350°F. Butter an 8-inch baking dish.

In a small bowl, mix together the flour, 1 cup sugar, the egg, butter, salt and baking powder.

In a medium bowl, combine the apricots and white chocolate, adjusting the amount of chocolate to balance the tartness of the apricots. If the apricots are very sweet, use the smallest amount of chocolate possible. If they are sour, use more. Place in the prepared dish and top with the crisp mixture. Bake until golden and the apricots are cooked, about 20 minutes. Let cool for 5 minutes.

Meanwhile, in a small saucepan over medium heat, combine the remaining 3 tablespoons sugar with 2 tablespoons water and the lavender and bring to a boil. Cook for 3 minutes, then strain the syrup through a fine sieve into a medium bowl, discarding the lavender. Add the cream and beat to stiff peaks.

Divide the crisp among six dessert bowls. Top with the lavender cream and serve immediately.

STRAWBERRY & RHUBARB TART
MASQUERADING AS PIZZA

This is a playful take on the traditional strawberry rhubarb pie my grandmother used to make. Good crust was serious business to her and I think she might approve of this version. She might even crack a smile at the whimsical presentation.

SERVES 6

TART DOUGH
½ cup butter or lard, diced and chilled
1¼ cups pastry flour
1 tablespoon sugar
pinch of sea salt
2 cups strawberries, stems removed
½ cup raspberries
1 cup sliced rhubarb
¼ cup sugar
¼ cup shaved white chocolate
2 tablespoons julienned fresh basil

Preheat the oven to 350°F.

In a food processor, pulse the chilled butter, flour, sugar and salt several times. Add 2 tablespoons ice water and pulse again; the dough should come together without being too wet or dry. If necessary, add more ice water. Chill the dough for 2 hours.

In a saucepan over medium heat, cook 1½ cups of the strawberries with the raspberries, rhubarb and sugar until the berries have softened, about 7 minutes. Purée in a blender until very smooth. Strain through a fine sieve, return to the pan and cook over low heat until thickened. Let cool. Thinly slice the remaining ½ cup strawberries crosswise and set aside.

Sprinkle a work surface with flour. Roll the chilled dough to a 9-inch circle. Transfer to a baking sheet and spread the berry purée on top. Roll up the outer edge of the dough to resemble a pizza crust. Top the purée with the white chocolate and strawberry slices. Bake until the edges are golden, about 15 minutes.

Top the tart with basil, cut into six slices and serve.

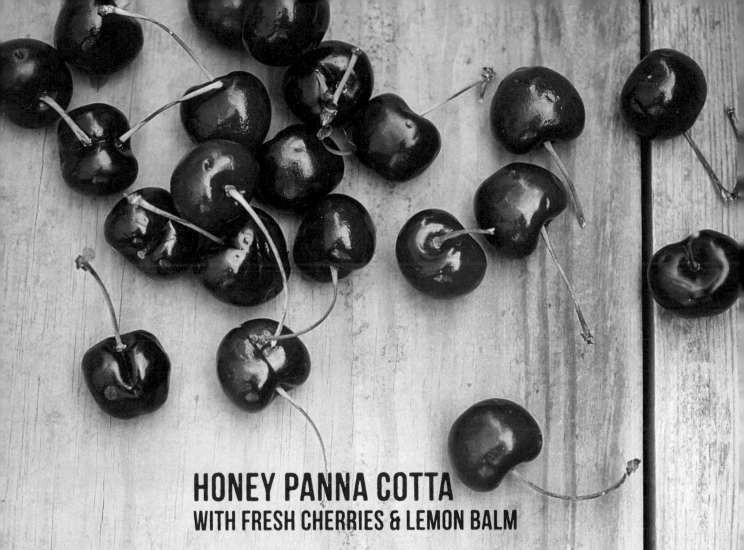

HONEY PANNA COTTA
WITH FRESH CHERRIES & LEMON BALM

I love to serve cherries unadorned. They are the perfect fruit with just the right balance of sweet and tart. In this dessert, they really shine, combining well with the floral notes of the lemon balm and the ultra-creamy panna cotta.

SERVES 4

1½ cups whole milk
½ cup heavy cream
⅓ cup plus 1 teaspoon sugar
¼ cup honey
sea salt
4 sheets of gelatin
¼ cup julienned lemon balm
1 teaspoon finely grated
    lemon zest
2 cups fresh cherries, pitted

In a small saucepan over medium heat, combine the milk, cream, ⅓ cup sugar, honey and a pinch of salt. Heat, stirring often, just until the sugar dissolves. Remove from the heat and add the gelatin, stirring continuously until it dissolves. Pour the milk mixture into four dessert bowls and chill in the refrigerator until fully set, about 2 hours.

In a small bowl, combine the lemon balm, 1 teaspoon sugar and zest and toss well. Divide among the set panna cotta. Top with the cherries and serve.

NAPOLEON OF RASPBERRIES
& ROSE-SCENTED MASCARPONE

The lingering, heady scent of wild roses was the inspiration for this dish. I wanted to capture the essence of roses in a way that was closer to the actual than what is found in rosewater (of which I'm not really a fan . . .). After a bit of research into perfume-making methods, I made an essence of roses that transports the flowers directly into this dish. This dessert clearly illustrates why the extra work is worth it. The dish is stunning.

SERVES 4

4 packed cups wild roses
1 cup plus 1 tablespoon brandy
8 ounces pâte feuilletée
   (see larder)
1¼ cups sugar
¼ cup pistachios, ground, plus
   2 tablespoons for garnish
1 cup mascarpone, at room
   temperature
sea salt
2 teaspoons finely grated
   orange zest
½ cup heavy cream
2 cups raspberries

In a small saucepan over low heat, combine half of the roses with 1 cup of the brandy and bring to a simmer. Remove from the heat and let stand for 2 hours while you prepare the pastry.

On a lightly floured surface, roll out the pâte feuilletée into a large rectangle. Trim the edges to make them even, then transfer the pastry onto a lightly buttered baking sheet. Prick the top all over with a fork, then sprinkle with ¼ cup each of the sugar and pistachios. Cover with a layer of parchment paper and place another equal-sized baking sheet on top, to keep the pastry flat. Chill in the refrigerator for at least 1 hour.

Preheat the oven to 400°F. Bake the pastry until golden, about 15 minutes. Cool on a wire rack, then cut the pastry into 8 strips, each measuring 1 x 6 inches. Set aside.

Strain the rose brandy through a fine sieve, pushing firmly to extract the liquid. Add ½ cup of the sugar and return to the stove. Simmer until it thickens, about 10 minutes.

Remove the petals from the remaining roses. In a food processor, combine the petals and the remaining ½ cup sugar. Process until smooth, about 2 minutes. Add the remaining 1 tablespoon brandy. Process 1 minute more.

In the bowl of a food processor, combine the mascarpone, salt to taste, orange zest and ¼ cup of the rose sugar. Process until smooth, about 2 minutes. With the motor running, add the cream in a thin stream and process for 1 minute more. Transfer to a pastry bag fitted with a medium star tip.

Top each of the pastry rectangles with the mascarpone. Gently press most of the raspberries into the mascarpone. Drizzle the raspberries with some rose syrup and then sprinkle with some of the ground pistachios. Double stack four of the pastries to make four napoleons.

Divide the napoleons among four dessert plates. Garnish with the remaining rose sugar, rose syrup, raspberries and pistachios. Serve immediately.

BASIL ICE CREAM
WITH SUMMER BERRIES

Basil might not seem to be a natural choice for dessert but take my word for it, it is. Basil's assertive fennel-like flavor becomes otherworldly once sweetened up. Here, I've paired it with simple ripe summer berries to make an unforgettably delicious dessert.

SERVES 4

2 cups heavy cream
2 cups whole milk
1 large egg
6 egg yolks
1 cup sugar
1 teaspoon vanilla extract
1 teaspoon molasses
2 cups fresh basil
2 ice cubes
2 tablespoons sunflower oil
pinch of sea salt
1 cup blackberries
1 cup raspberries

In a heavy-bottomed saucepan over low heat, whisk the cream, milk, egg and egg yolks, sugar, vanilla and molasses to combine. Cook, whisking often, until the cream begins to simmer. Pour through a fine sieve into a bowl and chill thoroughly in the refrigerator, at least 4 hours.

In a blender, combine the basil, ice, oil and salt. Blend until very smooth, about 1 minute. It should look like a green smoothie. Strain through a fine sieve into a small clear glass container and set aside for the ice to melt, about 20 minutes. The basil purée will float to the top of the mixture and separate from the water. Using a spoon, decant the basil purée off the top and into the chilled cream mixture and stir well to combine. Freeze in an ice cream maker per the manufacturer's directions. Transfer the ice cream to a metal or glass container and place in the freezer to harden, about 2 hours.

Scoop the ice cream into four chilled bowls. Top each with the berries. Serve immediately.

COOKING TIP
Smooth, creamy ice cream results from thousands of tiny ice crystals in each spoonful—each too small to feel on the tongue. Ice cream makers create this by mixing while they freeze but you can do the same by hand. Here's the trick: Pour the chilled ice cream mixture into a pre-frozen wide glass dish and place in the freezer until the mixture is very firm, stirring every 5 to 10 minutes to break up the forming ice crystals. Remember: the faster the chilling, the better the texture. Voila!

GRILLED PEACHES
WITH BUTTER PECAN ICE CREAM

Great peaches don't need much adornment to shine for dessert. I've warmed them on a grill to create a spectacular temperature and flavor contrast with this handmade butter pecan ice cream. The secret to great butter pecan ice cream is to allow the pecans to toast a bit in the butter, which turns into a bronze hue.

SERVES 4

1 cup pecans

3 tablespoons unsalted butter,
    plus 1 tablespoon melted

1 teaspoon sea salt

2 cups heavy cream

2 cups milk

6 egg yolks

1 large egg

1 cup sugar

1 teaspoon vanilla extract

1 teaspoon molasses

1 teaspoon freshly grated
    nutmeg

4 peaches, halved and pitted

In a medium sauté pan over medium heat, combine the pecans, 3 tablespoons butter and salt. Cook until the butter turns a golden hue and the nuts are toasted, about 4 minutes. Set aside to cool to room temperature.

In a heavy-bottomed saucepan over low heat, whisk together the cream, milk, egg yolks and egg, sugar, vanilla and molasses. Cook, whisking often, until the cream mixture begins to simmer. Strain through a fine sieve and chill thoroughly in the refrigerator, at least 4 hours or overnight.

Freeze in an ice cream maker per the manufacturer's directions (or see tip on page 214), then transfer the ice cream to a metal or glass container. Stir in the buttery pecans. Place the ice cream in the freezer to harden, about 2 hours.

Toss the peaches in the melted butter. Grill over a wood or charcoal fire, on a grill pan over high heat, or under a broiler until lightly charred and warmed through.

Place the peaches in four bowls. Top with scoops of the ice cream and serve immediately.

CARAMEL BRANDY-POACHED FIG TART
WITH CARAMEL ICE CREAM

I turn to flavors like caramel with its warming richness as the weather begins to cool and turn frosty. I love the temperature contrast in this dish when the tart is served right out of the oven. Warm brandied figs with slowly melting caramel ice cream are a revelation to eat on a blustery night.

SERVES 8

¼ cup julienned orange rinds

3 tablespoons sugar

2 tablespoons orange juice

4 cups dried figs, stems removed

1 cup brandy

2 cups white wine

1 pound tart dough (page 209)

caramel ice cream (see below)

Preheat the oven to 350°F and line a baking sheet with parchment paper.

In a small saucepan over high heat, combine the orange rinds and enough water to cover. Bring to a boil, then strain, discarding the water and returning the rinds to the pan with fresh water to cover. Repeat the blanching process until the rinds are no longer bitter, three or four times. Add the sugar and orange juice and boil until thickened. Set aside to cool.

In a small pot over high heat, combine the figs, brandy and wine and cook until the figs have softened. Set aside to cool.

Roll out the tart dough to a 10-inch circle. Transfer to the prepared baking sheet and brush the dough with the orange and fig syrups. Starting in the center of the dough, stand up the figs in a circular pattern and continue until all the figs are used up—the figs should make a circle in the center of the dough about 6 inches in diameter. Starting on an edge, roll up the sides of the dough toward the center. Rotate to an adjacent edge and continue rolling up the dough until the edge meets the fig filling. Firmly press the edge against the fig filling. Top the figs with the candied orange slices.

Bake in the oven until the crust is just golden, about 15 minutes.

Cut the tart into slices and divide among eight dessert plates. Top the warm tart slices with the caramel ice cream and serve immediately.

CARAMEL ICE CREAM

1¼ cups sugar

4 drops lemon juice

2¼ cups heavy cream

2 cups whole milk

6 egg yolks

1 large egg

1 teaspoon vanilla extract

1 teaspoon molasses

In a large saucepan over high heat, combine ½ cup of the sugar and the lemon juice with 2 tablespoons water and cook, without stirring, until the sugar turns very dark. Let cool for 2 minutes. Add ¼ cup of the cream and return to the heat. Heat on low, stirring constantly, until the sugar dissolves completely.

Add the remaining 2 cups cream, the milk, the remaining ¾ cup sugar, the egg yolks, egg, vanilla and molasses and whisk well. Cook, whisking often, until the mixture begins to simmer. Strain through a fine sieve and chill thoroughly in the refrigerator for at least 4 hours or overnight.

Freeze in an ice cream maker per the manufacturer's directions (or see tip on page 214), then transfer the ice cream to a metal or glass container. Place in the freezer to harden, about 2 hours.

PLUM CLAFLOUTI
WITH WARM CRÈME ANGLAISE

Clafouti is a classic country French farmhouse dessert that is both delicious and easy to make. True to form, we make this each fall when plums are in season. As for ease, I've taught my children how to make it and it is their contribution to our Sunday evening dinners. Preheating the heavy baking dish is essential to creating a light texture in the dessert.

SERVES 6

2 cups plums, halved and
    pitted
¾ cup sugar
2 cups whole milk
2 cups all-purpose flour
2 large eggs
2 teaspoons vanilla extract
1 teaspoon salt
confectioners' sugar

CRÈME ANGLAISE

3 egg yolks
½ cup heavy cream
½ cup milk
1 vanilla bean, split and
    scraped or freshly grated
    nutmeg to taste
¼ cup sugar
½ teaspoon molasses

Preheat the oven to 450°F.

Toss the plums in ¼ cup of the sugar.

In a blender, combine the milk, flour, the remaining ½ cup sugar, eggs, vanilla and salt. Blend until the mixture has no lumps of flour, about 2 minutes.

Place a 9-inch ovenproof baking dish in the oven until very hot, about 5 minutes. Working quickly, remove the dish from the oven and spray with non-stick cooking spray. Immediately pour the batter and plums into the dish. Return to the oven and bake until the clafouti is set and has risen, about 20 minutes.

Meanwhile, make the crème anglaise: In a small pot over low heat, combine the egg yolks, cream, milk, vanilla, sugar and molasses. Cook, stirring often, until the cream coats the back of a spoon. Pour through a fine-mesh sieve and set aside.

Remove the clafouti from the oven and dust with confectioners' sugar. Cut six slices of the clafouti and place on dessert plates. Top each with some crème Anglaise and serve immediately.

PLUMS

I like plums most of all stone fruits because, apart from being delicious and captivating, they are not flashy. In fact, this dowdy fruit flies mostly under the radar. The reason is simple: Plums never dominate when added to a dish. It is the perfect team player, simply adding a nice dose of bright acidity and sweetness but never stealing the show. When cooked, the flavors concentrate and become deeper. Plum halves, slowly dried in the oven (see the roasted ham on page 121), are heavenly with a buttery texture and a great sweet/sour balance. Puréed and then fully reduced into plum butter, they are magnificent.

PISTACHIO FINANCIER WITH PEAR & CHOCOLATE

Financier is the most regal of cakes, made with nut flours and lots of butter. As if it needed more, I've paired it here with poached pears and freshly grated bitter chocolate. The combination is stunning. Financier is best eaten fresh, still warm from the oven. Try freezing the leftovers, if you like (there rarely are any, though.)

SERVES 8

3 cups raw pistachios
1¼ cups all-purpose flour
2 cups sugar
1 teaspoon salt
½ pound unsalted butter, softened
4 large eggs
2 cups white wine
2 pieces star anise
1 cinnamon stick
2 cardamom pods
4 pears, peeled
1 cup chopped bittersweet chocolate or chocolate chips
pinch of ground nutmeg
pinch of ground cardamom
pinch of ground cinnamon
1 cup heavy cream
unsweetened chocolate, finely grated

Preheat the oven to 350°F. Butter a cake pan.

In the bowl of a food processor, combine the pistachios, flour and 1½ cups of the sugar and the salt. Process until very smooth.

In the bowl of an electric mixer fitted with a paddle attachment, whip the butter until light and fluffy, about 4 minutes. Stop the mixer and add the pistachio mix. Mix on low speed until incorporated, then increase the speed to medium. Add the eggs, one at a time, mixing until fully combined between each. Stop and scrape down the bowl if needed. The batter should be light and fluffy.

Transfer to the prepared cake pan and bake until set, about 20 minutes. Remove from the oven and cool.

In a medium stainless-steel saucepan over medium heat, combine the wine, spices, the remaining ½ cup sugar and the pears. Cook until the pears are just tender, about 10 minutes. Let the pears cool in the poaching liquid.

In a small saucepan over very low heat, combine the chocolate, the ground spices and half of the cream. Warm, stirring occasionally, until the chocolate is fully melted, about 5 minutes. Cool to room temperature.

In a medium bowl, beat the remaining cream with a whisk to stiff peaks. Add the whipped cream to the cooled chocolate and stir well.

Slice the cake with a sharp knife. Divide among eight dessert plates and top each slice with a dollop of the chocolate sauce. Slice the pears in half and divide the pieces among the plates. Sprinkle the grated chocolate on top of the pears and serve immediately.

PUMPKIN POUND CAKE
WITH CANDIED PEPITAS

Far superior for texture and flavor than the birthday standard, genoise layer cake, pound cake is my preferred cake style. Served warm from the oven with bits of smoky pumpkin, it captures the essence of autumn.

SERVES 8

2¼ cups sugar

4 drops lemon juice

1 cup toasted pumpkin seeds
  (pepitas)

2 teaspoons molasses

1 cup sliced pumpkin

1 tablespoon sunflower oil

pinch of ground clove

1 pound (4 sticks) unsalted
  butter, softened, plus more
  for greasing

4 cups all-purpose flour

3 teaspoons baking powder

1 teaspoon salt

2 teaspoons freshly grated
  nutmeg

4 large eggs

1½ cups crème Anglaise
  (see page 218)

In a small copper pot over high heat, combine ¼ cup sugar with the lemon juice and 2 tablespoons water and cook, without stirring, until the sugar begins to color, about 15 minutes. Let cool until it thickens to the consistency of honey.

Line a baking sheet with a silicone baking mat or parchment paper. Top with the pumpkin seeds. Lightly drizzle the cooled sugar syrup over the pumpkin seeds to coat them. Cool completely, then break the pepita candy into pieces. Set aside.

Preheat the oven to 450°F.

In a small bowl, combine 1 tablespoon warm water with the molasses and stir until the molasses dissolves. Toss in the pumpkin, oil and clove. Transfer to a baking sheet and roast until the pumpkin is tender and the edges begin to brown, about 10 minutes. Remove from the oven and set aside.

Reduce the oven temperature to 350°F. Grease a 10-inch cake pan with butter. In a medium bowl, whisk together the flour, baking powder, salt and 1 teaspoon of the nutmeg.

In the bowl of an electric mixer fitted with a paddle attachment, combine the softened butter and remaining 2 cups sugar. Beat at medium speed until lightened in color, then increase the speed to high and beat until the butter is light and fluffy, about 4 minutes. Add the eggs, one at a time, beating fully between each. Reduce the speed to low and add the flour mixture. Stir until just combined. Do not overmix.

Fill the cake pan with the batter and bake until a toothpick inserted in the center comes out clean, about 35 minutes. Cool before removing the cake from the pan.

In a small pot over low heat, warm the crème anglaise. Stir in the remaining teaspoon nutmeg.

Slice the cake and place on eight dessert plates. Garnish with the roasted pumpkin, candied pepitas and warm anglaise sauce.

WOODCUTTER'S TABLEAU IN GINGERBREAD

While making gingerbread men with my children on Christmas morning, we decided to tell the stories of what each one was doing and decorate them accordingly. There were football players, pirate captains and a princess, too. But it was the woodcutter that inspired this dessert.

SERVES 8

2 cups all-purpose flour

2 teaspoons baking powder

2 tablespoons freshly grated ginger

1 teaspoon freshly grated nutmeg

1 tablespoon ground cinnamon

½ teaspoon ground clove

1 cup unsalted butter

1¼ cups plus 2 tablespoons sugar

3 tablespoons molasses

2 large eggs

¼ cup dried cranberries

1 tablespoon grated orange zest

2 drops lemon juice

½ cup heavy cream

2 tablespoons confectioners' sugar, plus more for dusting

½ teaspoon vanilla extract

gingerbread cookies (page 224)

1 tablespoon melted chocolate

butter toffee logs (page 224)

Preheat the oven to 350°F. Butter the insides of 6 ramekins or other small baking dishes. Lightly coat with flour, then tap each lightly to remove the excess.

In a medium bowl, stir together the flour, baking powder, ginger and spices.

In the bowl of an electric mixer fitted with a paddle attachment, combine the butter, 1 cup of the sugar and the molasses. Mix on high speed until light and fluffy, about 4 minutes. Reduce the speed to medium and add the eggs, one at a time, fully incorporating after each. Reduce the speed to low and add the flour mixture. Mix until just combined.

Spoon the batter into the prepared ramekins set on a baking sheet. Bake until a toothpick inserted in the center comes out clean, 15 to 20 minutes. Let cool.

In a small saucepan over high heat, combine the cranberries, 2 tablespoons sugar, ¼ cup water and the orange zest and cook until the water is absorbed and the cranberries are soft, about 5 minutes. Set aside to cool.

In a heavy-bottomed copper saucepan (see tip, page 224) over high heat, combine the remaining ¼ cup sugar with 1 tablespoon water and the lemon juice and cook until the sugar boils and just begins to turn golden, about 10 minutes.

Cool the sugar until it has the consistency of honey. Using a teaspoon, drizzle onto a nonstick, silicone baking mat or parchment paper into the shape of an axe. Continue until all of the sugar is used up. As the axes are fragile, make extras to account for breakage.

In a medium bowl, combine the cream, confectioners' sugar and vanilla and whisk vigorously until you get firm peaks.

Gently dip the feet of the gingerbread cookies into the melted chocolate. Stand the gingerbread man up on a dessert plate, propping the cookie up with a small cup or suitable container. Once the chocolate has cooled the gingerbread man will stand on his own and the cup can be removed. Repeat until all of the cookies are used up.

Place a warmed gingerbread cake near the standing gingerbread man and top each cake with the sugar axes. Build a "fire" of toffee logs and cranberries near the gingerbread cake. Scatter the remaining toffee logs near the woodcutter. Place a dollop or two of whipped cream on the plate. Dust the plate with confectioners' sugar and serve immediately.

ERIC'S GRANDMOTHER'S GINGERBREAD COOKIES

2 cups all-purpose flour
½ teaspoons baking powder
½ teaspoon sea salt
2 teaspoons ground ginger
2 teaspoons ground cinnamon
½ teaspoon ground clove
½ teaspoon ground cardamom
¾ cup unsalted butter,
   softened
1 cup sugar
1 teaspoon vanilla extract
2 tablespoons molasses
1 large egg

Preheat the oven to 350°F. Lightly butter a baking sheet.

In a medium bowl, stir together the flour, baking powder, salt and spices.

In the bowl of an electric mixer fitted with a paddle attachment, combine the butter, sugar, vanilla and molasses. Mix on high speed until light and fluffy, about 4 minutes. Reduce the speed to medium, add the egg and mix until fully incorporated. Reduce the speed to low and add the flour mixture. Mix until just combined.

On a lightly floured work surface, roll the dough thinly. Cut the dough into shapes using a large gingerbread-man cookie cutter. Using a flat spatula, transfer to the prepared baking sheet. Continue until all of the dough is used up.

Bake the cookies until set, about 8 minutes. Cool the cookies before removing from the pan. They will keep in a covered container for 1 week (unless my kids or I are there, in which case 10 minutes, tops.)

BUTTER TOFFEE LOGS

1 cup sugar
2 drops lemon juice
pinch of sea salt
¼ cup butter

In a heavy-bottomed copper saucepan (see tip) over high heat, combine the sugar, lemon juice and 2 tablespoons water and cook until the sugar boils and begins to turn brown, about 10 minutes. Remove from the heat.

Add the salt and butter and stir constantly until the butter is fully melted and combined. Pour the mixture onto a buttered marble slab or heavy counter and stir continuously until cooled.

Form the toffee into a 1 by 5-inch rectangles, about ¼ of an inch thick. Using a sharp, buttered knife, slice the toffee on the bias into ¼-inch-thick slices and transfer the toffee slices onto a piece of wax paper, making sure that they do not touch each other. The toffee is at its best the day it is made but will keep for a week in a covered container at room temperature.

COOKING TIP

I suggest using copper pots when cooking the sugar in the recipes above because the copper helps to keep the sugar from re-crystallizing at high temperatures. If you don't have copper pots, a VERY clean stainless-steel pan will work with an additional drop or two of lemon juice.

WARM MADELEINES SCENTED WITH BERGAMOT

Bergamots are a type of highly aromatic orange grown in southern Italy with a scent that has long been used to perfume Earl Grey tea. As the warm madeleines, a type of soft cookie, come out of the oven, I brush the tops with a little Bergamot syrup. It is simply heaven.

SERVES 12

1 Bergamot orange, sliced
3 cups sugar
4 cups all-purpose flour
3 teaspoons baking powder
1 teaspoon salt
1 pound unsalted butter, at room temperature, plus more for greasing
4 large eggs

Preheat the oven to 350°F. Grease a large madeleine baking tray with butter.

In a small saucepan over high heat, cover the bergamot with water and bring to a boil. Strain through a colander, discarding the water. Return the bergamot to the pan and add fresh water. Blanch three or four times, until only a slight amount of the bitterness remains. Return the bergamot to the pan and add 1 cup of the sugar and ½ cup additional water. Cook until the sugar boils, about 3 minutes. Remove from the heat and set aside.

In a medium bowl, combine the flour, baking powder and salt and whisk well.

In the bowl of a stand mixer fitted with a paddle, combine the butter with the remaining 2 cups sugar. Beat at medium speed until the butter lightens in color. Increase the speed to high and beat until light and fluffy, about 4 minutes. Add the eggs, one at a time, beating fully between each. Reduce the speed to low and add the flour mixture and stir until just combined. Do not overmix.

Fill the madeleine tray with spoonfuls of the batter. Bake until firm to the touch, 8 to 10 minutes. Transfer to a platter and immediately brush the tops with the bergamot syrup. Repeat the process until the batter is used up.

Serve immediately.

CARROT CAKE
WITH CARROT CONFITURE & MASCARPONE

Carrots are a mainstay of the farm. They find their way into our wintertime desserts when fresh fruits are harder to come by. Here is a fun variation on carrot cake that takes notes from the flavors in gingersnap cookies.

SERVES 8

1 teaspoon plus 2 tablespoons grated fresh ginger

4 drops white vinegar

2½ cups plus 2 tablespoons sugar

sea salt

12 baby carrots, sliced thinly

1 cup mascarpone cheese

½ vanilla bean, split and scraped

1 teaspoon plus 3 tablespoons molasses

freshly grated nutmeg to taste

1 pound carrots, trimmed and washed

4 large eggs

1 cup sunflower oil

3 cups all-purpose flour

1 tablespoon baking powder

½ teaspoon allspice

1 tablespoon ground cinnamon

1 teaspoon ground cardamom

½ teaspoon ground clove

In a small saucepan over high heat, combine 1 teaspoon of the ginger, the vinegar, ½ cup of the sugar, a pinch of salt, and the baby carrots with ¼ cup water. Boil until the carrots are just tender. Set the confiture aside to cool.

In the bowl of an electric mixer fitted with a whisk attachment, combine the mascarpone, vanilla, 1 teaspoon of the molasses, the nutmeg and 2 tablespoons sugar. Beat on high speed until light and fluffy. Transfer to a container and chill in the refrigerator.

Preheat the oven to 350°F. Grease the inside of a 10-inch cake pan.

Using the small side of a box grater, grate the carrots into a large bowl. Add the remaining 2 tablespoons grated ginger, 3 tablespoons molasses, the eggs, 2 cups sugar, the oil and 1½ teaspoons of salt and mix well.

In a large bowl, whisk together the flour, baking powder and spices. Add to the carrot mixture and stir until just combined. Do not overmix.

Fill the prepared cake pan with the batter and bake until a toothpick inserted into the center comes out clean, about 20 minutes.

Remove from the oven and cool. Once cool, cut the cake into eight slices.

Divide the cake slices among eight dessert plates. Garnish with the mascarpone and carrot confiture and serve immediately.

THE LARDER

ONE OF THE SECRETS TO COOKING SEASONALLY FROM THE GARDEN IS THE USE OF "BUILDING BLOCK" RECIPES. THESE ARE QUICK RECIPES THAT CAN BE MADE AHEAD AND PLAY AN IMPORTANT ROLE IN MAKING A GREAT DISH. ROASTED GARLIC AND ROASTED GARLIC OIL, OR A GOOD ALL-PURPOSE VINAIGRETTE, HAVE A MUCH GREATER EFFECT THAN THE EFFORT NEEDED TO MAKE THEM. OFTENTIMES, THESE RECIPES ARE THE "GLUE" THAT CAN HOLD A COLLECTION OF FRESH PRODUCE TOGETHER AND TURN IT INTO A MEMORABLE MEAL.

ROASTED GARLIC & ROASTED GARLIC OIL

This recipe produces both roasted garlic and richly flavored garlic oil. If the dish you are making calls for puréed garlic, transfer the cloves to a food processor while still hot, which results in a very smooth purée. The leftover oil from this recipe is garlic infused and delicious. I call for it in many recipes.

MAKES ¾ CUP

1 cup garlic cloves, peeled
1 cup sunflower oil

In a small saucepan over medium heat, cook the garlic and oil until the garlic turns golden and softens, about 25 minutes. Using a hand strainer, remove the garlic and strain the oil. Store separately in airtight containers for 7 days in the refrigerator.

HANDMADE VINEGAR

MAKES ABOUT 3 CUPS

½ cup Bragg's unpasteurized apple cider vinegar

¾ bottle of red or white wine

Pour the vinegar into the wine bottle, close the top and shake well to combine. Remove the top from the wine and set the bottle in a dark place at room temperature.

Shake the bottle to mix and aerate every 4 days. The wine will turn to vinegar in about 3 weeks. Pour 1 cup of this vinegar into a new bottle of wine to continue the process.

Handmade vinegar keeps indefinitely and is a good way to use up unfinished wine.

BASIC VINAIGRETTE

This simple vinaigrette is indispensable in my kitchen. It makes everything it touches taste better. Asparagus taste more vividly of asparagus. On lettuces, its lightness lets the individual leaves retain their distinct flavors. Why not use olive oil? While I love it, it makes everything it touches taste like olive oil, instead of letting the ingredients shine.

MAKES ABOUT 1 CUP

1 cup sunflower oil
2 tablespoons red wine vinegar

½ garlic clove, crushed
1 teaspoon sea salt

In a container with a tight-fitting lid, combine the oil, vinegar, garlic and salt. Seal the container and shake vigorously, like a bartender would shake a cocktail. Immediately pour out the desired amount of vinaigrette—typically that is a few tablespoons for a salad that serves four. This vinaigrette separates quickly, so re-shake to combine between uses if it stands longer than 15 seconds.

WHOLE-GRAIN MUSTARD VINAIGRETTE

MAKES ABOUT 1 CUP

1 cup basic vinaigrette (see above)

2 teaspoons whole-grain mustard

In a container with a tight-fitting lid, combine the vinaigrette and mustard. Seal the container and shake vigorously to combine the ingredients.

TRADITIONAL AÏOLI

Aioli is simply mayonnaise with lots of garlic and lemon added. It is the epitome of a building block recipe as it can be used in literally hundreds of other cold sauces.

MAKES ABOUT 3 CUPS

¼ cup roasted garlic (see opposite)	2 tablespoons lemon juice
½ to 1 clove garlic, minced	1 tablespoon Dijon mustard
1 large egg yolk	1 teaspoon sea salt
	2 cups sunflower oil

In the bowl of a food processor or blender, combine both the roasted and fresh garlics with the egg yolk, lemon juice, mustard and salt and 2 tablespoons water. Blend on high speed for 30 seconds. With the motor running, slowly drizzle in the oil until fully incorporated. Taste for seasoning and adjust if necessary. This will keep for 4 days in the fridge.

TAPENADE

MAKES ABOUT ½ CUP

1 cup Kalamata or niçoise olives, pitted	1 teaspoon grated lemon zest
½ clove garlic, minced	1 to 2 tablespoons olive oil
1 tablespoon minced red onion	lemon juice

In the bowl of a food processor, combine the olives, garlic, onion, lemon zest and olive oil. Pulse to chop the olives coarsely and mix the ingredients. Season to taste with the lemon juice. Transfer to a clean container with a tight-fitting lid and keep in the refrigerator for 2 weeks.

PICKLED GINGER

MAKES ½ CUP

4 ounces fresh ginger, peeled	¼ cup white vinegar
1 cup unseasoned rice vinegar	2 tablespoons sugar

In a small saucepan over high heat, boil the ginger in 3 cups water for 10 minutes. Remove from the heat and drain. Using a thin, sharp knife or mandoline, slice the ginger crosswise into very thin slices. Transfer to a small heatproof bowl.

In a small saucepan over high heat, cook both vinegars and the sugar until the sugar has dissolved and the vinegar simmers. Pour the hot vinegar over the ginger. Transfer to a container and store in the refrigerator for up to 4 weeks.

ALMOND TARATOR

Emulsified to a rich thickness like aïoli, tarator uses no eggs. This classic Turkish sauce makes a spectacular addition to warm poached shrimp or roasted vegetables like cauliflower. Pistachios can be substituted for the almonds for a nutty change.

MAKES 2 CUPS

1 cup toasted almonds	¼ cup sunflower oil
2 tablespoons roasted garlic (page 230)	sea salt

In a food processor, combine the nuts, garlic and 2 tablespoons water. Process on high speed until very smooth, scraping the sides of the bowl if necessary.

With the motor running, slowly add the oil until fully incorporated. Season with the salt. Store in a tightly covered container in the fridge for 4 days.

SMOKED SALT

This recipe is impractical to make on its own but we'll often put a dish of salt in the corner of our smoker when smoking other dishes. The salt takes on a wonderful smoky quality that we use to finish other dishes.

MAKES 1 CUP

1 cup sea salt
fruitwood for smoking

Put the salt in a low, flat heatproof container and set it in a smoker. Prepare a wood fire for smoking and smoke the salt for at least 2 hours.

OVEN-DRIED TOMATOES

We make these tomatoes at the end of the night in the restaurant. Taking advantage of the still hot, but slowly cooling ovens, the tomatoes cook and dry gently through the night. Alternatively, you could set your oven to its lowest warming setting to gently bake.

MAKES 4 CUPS

4 cups roma or other salad tomatoes
1 tablespoon olive oil
2 teaspoons sea salt

Preheat the oven to 400°F for at least 15 minutes prior to making this recipe.

Quarter the tomatoes and remove any remaining stems. Toss in a medium bowl with the oil and salt.

Transfer the tomatoes to a baking sheet lined with parchment paper. Place in the oven, turn the oven off and leave them inside overnight.

The following day, transfer the tomatoes to a clean container and cool in the refrigerator. These will keep for up to 4 days.

TOMATO POWDER

This recipe requires the use of a food dehydrator. Alternatively, substitute packaged dried tomatoes for the fresh.

MAKES ¾ CUP

4 cups roma tomatoes

Slice the tomatoes and transfer to the drying racks of a food dehydrator set to 140°F. Dehydrate the tomatoes until brittle and very dry. Break up the dried tomatoes into small pieces and transfer them to a blender. Purée in the blender until very smooth, about 3 minutes.

TOMATO FONDUTO

With its concentrated flavor, this thick tomato purée instantly adds life to any dish. In the late summer, we make large batches to use up the last of the tomatoes; if doing so, try baking the purée in the oven to keep the fonduto from burning.

MAKES 1 CUP

4 shallots, peeled and sliced
1 tablespoon sunflower oil
8 roma tomatoes, sliced
2 bay laurel leaves
sea salt and freshly ground black pepper

In a medium pot over medium heat, cook the shallots in the oil until they just begin to color, about 10 minutes. Add the tomatoes and bay leaves and cook until the juice from the tomatoes has reduced and the tomatoes have thickened, about 45 minutes.

Discard the bay leaves and transfer the tomato mixture to a blender. Purée at high speed until very smooth, about 5 minutes. Season with salt and pepper.

BALSAMIC ONIONS

This recipe falls into the "don't judge a book by its cover" category. While the outer peels of the onion will look burned, the inner layers are an absolute delight! I discovered this method purely by accident when I left onions in the oven to roast for too long.

MAKES 1 TO 2 CUPS

1 large onion
1 tablespoon balsamic
    vinegar

1 tablespoon olive oil
sea salt and freshly
    ground black pepper

Preheat oven to 400°F.

Leaving the onion unpeeled, quarter it and transfer to a medium bowl. Add the vinegar and oil and sprinkle with salt and pepper. Toss to coat well.

Transfer to a baking sheet lined with parchment paper and bake until the onions are deeply colored and very tender, about 20 minutes.

Peel away the outer 2 or 3 layers of the onion and discard. The inner portions will be perfectly roasted and richly flavored. Use immediately.

SALTED LEMONS

I love to have salted lemons on hand to add to such recipes as heirloom carrots confit on page 67 or the risotto cakes on page 192.

MAKES 3 CUPS

5 lemons, halved
2 cups sea salt
2 tablespoons sugar

In a glass container, layer the lemons, salt and sugar and place in the refrigerator for 10 days.

Remove the lemons from the salt and rinse lightly. Store in a clean container in the refrigerator for up to 2 days.

DUCK LEG CONFIT

To make a confit, fat must be rendered. I mix diced fat with an equal amount of water and cook it gently until the water has just cooked out. Keep the temperature low, otherwise the rendered fat will take on a "cooked" flavor. In a pinch, I've made a confit with olive oil, the key is keep it from getting too hot. (Delicious with olives, rosemary and gnocchi!)

MAKES 6 CUPS

6 duck legs
sea salt
4 cups duck fat, melted

1 cinnamon stick
1 orange, halved

Preheat the oven to 200°F.

Season the duck legs liberally with salt and place in a heavy-bottomed braising pan. Add the fat, cinnamon and orange. Cook over medium heat until the fat begins to simmer.

Transfer the braising pan to the oven and cook until the duck legs are very tender, 4 to 5 hours. Remove the pan from the oven to cool. Store the cooked duck in the fat in the refrigerator for up to 2 weeks.

SHALLOT CONFIT

MAKES 1 CUP

6 shallots, peeled and
    sliced
1½ cups white wine
6 peppercorns

2 bay laurel leaves
1 tablespoon unsalted
    butter

In a small stainless-steel saucepan over high heat, combine the shallots, wine, peppercorns and bay leaves. Cook until the wine has fully reduced, about 15 minutes. Remove from the heat and stir in the butter. Store in the refrigerator for up to 2 weeks.

DUCK PROSCIUTTO

While this preparation requires very little work, it does require quite a bit of time, about 5 days. After curing the breasts, they can be air-dried, uncovered, in the fridge for an additional 2 weeks.

MAKES 2 POUNDS

2 boneless duck breasts with skin, 8 ounces each

1½ cups kosher salt

½ cup (packed) dark brown sugar

10 juniper berries

1 tablespoon coriander seeds

1 teaspoon freshly cracked black pepper

1 tablespoon orange zest

Using a small knife, trim excess fat from the sides of the breasts. Lightly score the remaining fat in a diamond pattern. In a medium bowl, toss together the remaining ingredients.

Arrange 2 sheets of plastic wrap side by side on a work surface. Spread 1 scant cup of the salt mixture (do not pack) in the center of each sheet, spreading it out to match the size of a duck breast. Top each with 1 breast, fat side down. Spread the remaining salt mixture over the meat, dividing equally. Bring the plastic wrap up and over each breast, wrapping it tightly. Place on a small, glass baking dish, fat side down, and refrigerate for 5 days to cure. The meat should be very firm to the touch and dark in color.

Unwrap the duck breasts. Remove the salt mixture and lightly rinse. Dry the duck thoroughly with paper towels. Using a long, sharp knife, thinly slice the meat.

SALT-CURED FOIE GRAS

This recipe requires three days to cure. Warming the foie gras to room temperature makes it easier to remove the veins.

MAKES 4 CUPS

1 lobe of foie gras, about 1½ pounds

1 pound sea salt, plus more for seasoning

½ cup sugar

2 tablespoons black peppercorns

2 tablespoons coriander seeds

2 tablespoons lemon zest

Split the lobe open and remove the veins and any discolored areas. Season lightly with salt. Transfer the liver to a large piece of cheesecloth and form into a 1½-inch-thick roll. Tightly roll up the cheesecloth and tie the ends to secure.

Mix together the salt and sugar. Put half in the bottom of a glass baking dish. Top with half of the peppercorns, coriander seeds and lemon zest. Place the foie gras on top and sprinkle with the remaining spices, then cover with the remaining salt mixture. Cure for 3 days in the fridge. Remove the roll from the salt and dry in the refrigerator for an additional day.

Unwrap the liver and shave with a peeler or very sharp knife. Serve immediately.

BASIL COULIS

MAKES ½ CUP

1 cup fresh basil

½ cup fresh parsley

2 ice cubes

¼ cup olive oil

2 tablespoons sunflower oil

sea salt

lemon juice to taste

In a blender, combine the herbs, ice and both oils. Blend on high speed until very smooth. Transfer to a small bowl. Season with the salt and lemon juice and use immediately.

GOOSE LIVER BUTTER

MAKES ABOUT 3 CUPS

½ pound goose liver,
   rinsed and cubed
2 tablespoons Calvados
1 teaspoon nutmeg
1 teaspoon pepper
1 teaspoon ground fennel

2 teaspoons sea salt
¼ cup roasted garlic
   (see page 230)
1½ cups (2 sticks)
   unsalted butter,
   softened

In a medium bowl, combine the liver, Calvados, spices and garlic. Cover and marinate in the fridge overnight.

Sauté the liver mixture with 1 tablespoon of the butter in a sauté pan over medium heat. Cook until the liver reaches 145°F. Let cool fully, then transfer to a food processor and purée until very smooth. Add the remaining butter and purée until fully combined.

On a clean work surface, spread a 24-inch length of plastic wrap. Place spoonfuls of the butter along the long edge of the plastic nearest you. Roll the butter and plastic over to form a log and gently compress to remove any air. Refrigerate for 2 hours or until firm and use within 2 weeks.

POACHED CHICKEN

MAKES 2 CUPS

2 boneless, skinless
   chicken breasts
sea salt

2 cups garlic oil
   (page 230)

Season the chicken with salt. In a medium saucepan over medium heat, cook the chicken and garlic oil until the oil just begins to simmer (180°F on a thermometer). Reduce the heat to low so that the chicken cooks at a bare simmer until just cooked through and no longer glassy inside, 20 to 30 minutes depending on the thickness of the breasts (160°F on a thermometer). Remove the pan from the heat to cool for 5 minutes. Then remove the chicken from the oil to cool fully. Chill in the fridge for up to 4 days.

CURRY POWDER

I love this combination of curry spices and add it to braised rabbit on page 130 and red lentil–crusted grouper on page 172.

MAKES ⅓ CUP

2 tablespoons ground
   cumin
2 tablespoons ground
   coriander
1 tablespoon ground
   mustard seeds
1 tablespoon ground
   fennel seeds

1 teaspoon ground
   cardamom
1 teaspoon ground
   fenugreek
1 teaspoon ground
   turmeric
½ teaspoon ground
   cinnamon
¼ teaspoon ground
   nutmeg

In a sauté pan over low heat, combine all of the spices. Cook, stirring constantly, until the spices are very fragrant, 3 to 4 minutes. Remove the pan from the heat and store the spices in a container with a tight-fitting lid for up to 4 weeks.

BEEF (OR PORK) STOCK

Every chef has his own stock recipe but they are basically rooted in the same equation: bones plus vegetables plus spice. For a lamb stock, use this same recipe substituting lamb bones for the beef and pork and losing the portobello mushrooms. For rabbit stock, see page 130. All the following stocks keep for 2 months in the freezer.

MAKES 8 CUPS

1 pound beef or pork bones
1 onion, quartered
2 large carrots, chopped
2 portobello mushrooms

2 stalks celery, chopped
2 tablespoons sunflower oil
1 tablespoon black peppercorns

Preheat the oven to 400°F.

On a baking sheet, roast the bones in the oven until mahogany in color, about 25 minutes. Transfer to a stockpot and add about 10 cups water to cover the bones. Bring to a boil, then reduce the heat to a bare simmer for 1 hour.

Meanwhile, in a large bowl, toss the vegetables in the oil to evenly coat. Transfer to a baking sheet and roast in the oven until the edges of the vegetables just begin to brown, about 20 minutes. Transfer to the stockpot, add the peppercorns and cook for an additional 30 minutes. Strain the stock through a fine sieve before using. Chill for up to 7 days in the fridge.

FISH STOCK

MAKES 8 CUPS

1 onion, quartered
2 large carrots, chopped
2 stalks of celery, chopped
2 tablespoons sunflower oil

2 pounds fish bones and skins
1 tablespoon black peppercorns
4 bay laurel leaves

Preheat the oven to 400°F.

In a large bowl, toss the vegetables in the oil to evenly coat.

Transfer to a baking sheet and roast in the oven until the edges of the vegetables just begin to brown, about 20 minutes. Transfer the vegetables to a stockpot and add the fish bones and skins, peppercorns and bay leaves. Add 8 to 10 cups water to cover the bones and vegetables and bring to a boil. Reduce the heat to a bare simmer and cook for an additional 30 minutes.

Strain the stock through a fine strainer before using. Chill for up to 4 days in the fridge.

CHICKEN (OR DUCK) STOCK

MAKES 8 CUPS

1 pound chicken or duck bones
1 onion, quartered
1 large carrot

2 stalks celery
1 tablespoon black peppercorns

Preheat the oven to 400°F.

Place the bones and vegetables on a baking sheet and roast in the oven until the bones just begin to color, about 20 minutes. Transfer the bones to a stockpot, add 8 to 10 cups water to just cover the bones and bring to a boil over high heat. Reduce the heat to a bare simmer and cook for 40 minutes.

Add the vegetables and peppercorns and simmer for an additional 30 minutes. Strain through a fine sieve before using. Chill for up to 5 days in the fridge.

VEGETABLE STOCK

MAKES 8 CUPS

2 onions, quartered
2 large carrots, chopped
2 portobello mushrooms
2 stalks celery, chopped

2 tablespoons sunflower
  oil
1 tablespoon black
  peppercorns
2 bay laurel leaves

Preheat the oven to 400°F. In a large bowl, toss together the vegetables with the oil to evenly coat.

Transfer to a baking sheet and roast in the oven until the edges of the vegetables just begin to brown, about 20 minutes. Transfer to a stockpot and add 8 to 10 cups water to cover the vegetables. Add the peppercorns and bay leaves and bring to a boil, then reduce the heat to a bare simmer. Cook for 30 minutes and strain through a fine sieve before using.

PASTA DOUGH

MAKES 2 POUNDS

8 cups bread flour
12 large eggs
1 tablespoon sea salt

In the bowl of a stand mixer fitted with a dough hook, combine the flour, eggs and salt. Mix on low speed until the mixture forms a very firm dough. Continue to mix the dough until very smooth.

Transfer the dough from the mixer to a floured work surface. Cut into 4 equal portions, wrap in plastic wrap and store in the refrigerator for 2 days or in the freezer for 4 weeks.

PÂTÉ FEUILLETÉE

This foolproof puff pastry recipe is for the Napoleon on page 213, but it's also divine enclosed around fillings like beef and mushrooms, salmon, or soft-ripened cheese like Camembert.

MAKES 2 POUNDS

2 cups all-purpose flour
2 cups cake or pastry
  flour
1½ teaspoons sea salt

2 tablespoons sugar
1 cup (2 sticks) unsalted
  butter, diced
1 teaspoon lemon juice

In a large bowl, stir together the flours, salt and sugar. Stir in the pieces of butter so that each one is completely coated in flour. Combine 1 cup very cold water with the lemon juice; stir into the bowl, lightly tossing the flours and sugar to moisten evenly. Gather the dough into a shaggy dough ball.

On a lightly floured surface, roll out the dough to form a rectangle about ½ inch thick. Square the edges, then fold the dough into thirds like a business letter, wrap in plastic and refrigerate for at least 30 minutes.

Place the chilled dough on the floured work surface and turn at a 90-degree angle from the last time you rolled it out. Roll into a rectangle again and fold into thirds. If the dough is still cold and manageable, rotate and roll again, then fold into thirds, or refrigerate and continue in 30 minutes. Finish by rolling the dough out to the size of a baking sheet. Place on a lightly floured baking sheet and wrap in plastic. Refrigerate for at least 30 minutes.

Roll out the dough to ¼-inch thickness and cut into shapes with a sharp knife. Use as directed in recipes calling for puff pastry, or alternatively, enclose desired fillings and bake in a preheated 400°F oven until puffed and golden brown, about 20 minutes.

INDEX